Embedded Ins General Education Classroom for Students with Intellectual and Developmental Disabilities

Prism Series Vol. 12

J. Matt Jameson
John McDonnell
Tim Riesen
Shamby Polychronis

Council for Exceptional Children

DADD
Division on Autism and Developmental Disabilities

© 2020 by Council for Exceptional Children
All rights reserved.

No part of this publication may be reproduced, stored in a retrieval system, or transmitted, in any form or by any means, electronic, mechanical, photocopying, recording, or otherwise, without prior written permission of the copyright owner.

Council for Exceptional Children
3100 Clarendon Blvd, Suite 600
Arlington, VA 22201-5332
www.cec.sped.org

Library of Congress Cataloging-in-Publication data

Jameson, J. Matt
Embedded Instruction in the General Education Classroom for Students with Intellectual and Developmental Disabilities / J. Matt Jameson, John McDonnell, Tim Riesen, and Shamby Polychronis

p. cm.
Includes biographical references.

ISBN 978-0-86586-545-7 (soft cover edition)
ISBN 978-0-86586-546-4 (eBook edition)
CEC Product No. P6322 (soft cover edition)

Cover design by Tom Karabatakis, Tompromo Marketing

Layout by Tom Karabatakis, Tompromo Marketing

Printed in the United States of America by Gasch Printing

First edition

10 9 8 7 6 5 4 3 2 1

Contents

About the Authors v

About the Prism Series vii

Chapter 1
Embedded Instruction in General Education Classrooms 1

Chapter 2
Preparing for Instruction 9

Chapter 3
Designing an Embedded Instruction Program 21

Chapter 4
Implementing the Embedded Instruction Program 39

Chapter 5
Supporting Student Learning 45

References 55

Appendices
    Appendix A: Forms 61
    Appendix B: Peer Tutoring Training Script 67
    Appendix C: Annotated Bibliography of Embedded Instruction Research 74

About the Authors

J. Matt Jameson is Associate Professor of Special Education at the University of Utah. His primary research interests include instructional strategies and inclusive educational procedures for students with significant cognitive disabilities. He has authored and co-authored articles and book chapters focused on providing students with disabilities a free and appropriate public education and highly qualified special education teachers, instructional strategies to support students with significant cognitive disabilities in inclusive settings, and evaluations of distance education and teacher preparation programs. He served as the Distance Education Coordinator for the University of Utah's Department of Special Education from 2004 to 2018 and has been involved in the design and delivery of distance education courses since 2000. He is currently the program coordinator for the Low Incidence Disability Program. He has taught numerous on-campus and distance education courses including an ongoing involvement with the support of distance education students. In addition, he worked as a classroom teacher for middle school students with significant cognitive disabilities and for preschoolers with autism spectrum disorder, and as a specialist in a residential program for adults with significant cognitive disabilities.

John McDonnell is Professor in the Department of Special Education at the University of Utah. His research agenda focuses on the development and validation of curriculum and instructional strategies to support students with severe disabilities in inclusive educational and community environments. Over the last 30 years, he has designed and implemented a number of single-subject, group, and correlational studies examining educational methods and models for individuals with disabilities. These studies have addressed areas such as the effectiveness of embedded instruction for students with severe disabilities enrolled in general education classes, comparisons of inclusive and segregated education placements for students with severe disabilities, and large-scale regression studies identifying the components of education and supported employment models that predict employment and community-living outcomes for youth and adults with disabilities. Dr. McDonnell's work has been published in a number of internationally and nationally recognized journals including *Exceptional Children, Education and Training in Autism and Developmental Disabilities, Intellectual and Developmental Disabilities, Career Development for Exceptional Individuals,* and the *Journal of Applied Behavior Analysis*. In addition, he is the author or co-author of six books. Dr. McDonnell has obtained over $16 million in federal and state funding to support his research and outreach activities.

Tim Riesen is a research assistant professor with a joint appointment in the Center for Persons with Disabilities and the Department of Special Education and Rehabilitation at Utah State University. His research focuses on promoting positive employment outcomes for individuals with significant disabilities, secondary transition, policy, and evidence-based instruction. He has published articles on customized employment, transition to employment, inclusive education, instruction in applied community settings, distance education, alternatives to guardianship, and interagency collaboration.

Shamby Polychronis is a professor in the Education Department at Westminster College, Salt Lake City. She has served on multiple grant projects, co-authored several articles, and presented at state and national conferences. Her scholarly interests include postschool outcomes for students, family support services, and teacher education. Dr. Polychronis teaches courses on the disability rights movement, autism spectrum disorder (debunking myths and stereotypes), inclusive education practices, and effective methodologies for individualizing instruction. She advocates for social justice issues including alternatives to guardianship, full inclusion in school and community environments, eliminating aversive interventions, and meaningful employment. In 2018, she received Westminster College's Gore Excellence in Teaching Award.

About the Prism Series

The Prism series, developed by the Council for Exceptional Children (CEC) Division on Autism and Developmental Disabilities (DADD) and co-published with CEC, is a collection of volumes that highlight evidence-based research-to-practice teaching strategies and interventions geared toward supporting students with autism spectrum disorder, intellectual disability, and other developmental disabilities. The volumes in the Prism collection address interventions in the classroom, home, and community and focus on how to help students build needed skills.

The Board of Directors of DADD is pleased to offer its 12th publication in the Prism series, *Embedded Instruction in the General Education Classroom for Students With Intellectual and Developmental Disabilities.* This volume focuses on the important practice of embedded instruction for students with intellectual and developmental disabilities in general education settings. We thank Drs. Jameson, McDonnell, Riesen, and Polychronis for authoring this volume and are confident that readers will find the information it contains to be of significant value.

—Michael L. Wehmeyer, Prism Series Executive Editor and Chair, DADD Publications Committee

DADD 2018 Board of Directors

Michael Wehmeyer
President and Publications Committee Chair

Ginevra Courtade
President-Elect

Robert Pennington
Vice-President

Gardner Umbarger
Treasurer

Angi Stone-MacDonald
Secretary and Awards Committee Chair

Teresa Taber Doughty
Executive Director

Jordan Shurr
Immediate Past-President

Kimberly Maich
Canadian Member

Nikki Murdick
Member-at-Large and Membership Committee Chair

Elizabeth Harkins
Member-at-Large and Diversity Committee Chair

Emily Bouck
Communication Committee Chair and Web Coordinator
Critical Issues/CAN Committee Chair

Cary Trump
Student Representative

Chris Denning
Newsletter Editor

Stan Zucker
Editor, *Education and Training in Autism and Developmental Disabilities*

CHAPTER 1

Embedded Instruction in General Education Classrooms

The number of students with intellectual and developmental disabilities (IDD) served in general education classes has increased over the last decade (Morningstar, Kurth, & Johnson, 2017). Research has consistently shown that inclusive educational programs produce positive educational and social outcomes for all students, both with and without disabilities (McDonnell & Hunt, 2014). However, including students with IDD in general education classes and ensuring they have access to the general education curriculum can present a number of challenges to teachers. Perhaps one of the most significant challenges is ensuring these students receive evidence-based instruction that is individualized and which is compatible with the typical activities and routines in general education classrooms (Ryndak, Orlando, & Burnett, in press). One strategy that has been shown to be particularly effective in addressing these two issues is embedded instruction (EI; Jimenez & Kamei, 2015; McDonnell, Jameson, Riesen, & Polychronis, 2014).

What Is Embedded Instruction?

A number of instructional approaches designed to distribute instructional trials within the ongoing routines and activities of classroom environments have been examined over the last several decades. Various labels—including *naturalistic instruction*, *incidental teaching*, and *embedded instruction*—have been used to differentiate these instructional approaches from the kind of discrete-trial instruction that often occurs in more traditional separate special education programs (Collins, 2012). For procedures used with school-age children in general education classes, we prefer the term *embedded instruction*. EI is characterized by several critical features:

- **The expected learning outcomes for the student in the general education class are clearly delineated.** The teacher has developed explicit goals and objectives for the student, and specific criteria for judging the effectiveness of EI on student learning have been established.
- **Instruction is designed to accommodate the presence or absence of "natural" instructional trials within typical routines or activities.** Prior to

instruction, the teacher analyzes the typical routines and activities of the general education class to identify when and how often opportunities to teach the target skill will occur naturally within the usual classroom routines or activities. If natural teaching opportunities occur inconsistently or without sufficient frequency, then the teacher identifies specific opportunities when supplemental instructional examples might be presented to the student to promote efficient learning.

- **Instructional trials are distributed within or across the typical routines or activities in the general education class.** In discrete-trial teaching arrangements, instructional trials typically are presented one after another within a teaching session (i.e., one-on-one massed practice). In contrast, EI trials are not massed but are distributed across naturally occurring opportunities in the routines and activities of the general education classroom.

- **The number and time of delivery of instructional trials is planned and scheduled within each routine and activity.** The teacher creates a schedule for the delivery of instructional trials that ensures sufficient opportunities for instruction and minimizes the disruption of classroom activities and interactions.

- **The teacher uses evidence-based instruction procedures.** The teacher utilizes response prompting and fading procedures that minimize errors during the initial stages of acquisition, corrects errors consistently, and builds on the natural reinforcers available within the classroom.

- **Instruction decisions are driven by student performance data.** Data on the student's acquisition, maintenance, and generalization of the targeted skills are collected regularly, with the teacher using these data to make modifications to the teaching plan in order to maximize its efficacy.

In this book, we provide step-by-step directions for designing and implementing EI with students with IDD in the general education classroom setting. This work is based on two assumptions. First, EI will only be effective if special and general educators collaborate to meet the education needs of the student. EI incorporates a number of teaching strategies that most special educators know about and use in other instructional settings. This knowledge is critical to the overall effectiveness of EI in meeting a student's needs. However, if EI is going to be used to maximize students' successful participation in the general education setting and the general education curriculum, the knowledge of general educators and their participation in the design and implementation of EI is critical to its success.

Second, EI should be viewed as only one small piece of a student's education program in general education classes. Other significant elements include the use of differentiated curriculum strategies, the use of adaptations and accommodations to allow the student to participate successfully in all instructional activities, and personal supports to allow full participation in the general education class (Hunt & McDonnell, 2007; McDonnell & Hunt, 2014; Ryndak et al., in press). In addition, many students also require direct instruction in traditional one-to-one or small-group formats. The challenge facing teachers is how to combine and integrate EI with other instruction strategies to help students succeed in school.

Implementing Embedded Instruction

The flowchart in Figure 1.1 outlines the basic steps of developing and implementing EI for a student enrolled in a general education class. The steps include (a) preparing for instruction, (b) designing the EI program, (c) implementing the program, and (d) supporting efficient student learning through data-based decision making. Each step is further divided into specific activities that teachers must complete in order to successfully implement EI.

Step 1: Prepare for Instruction

The first activity required to prepare for EI is to identify the learning goals and objectives for the student's participation in the general education class. These goals and objectives can be obtained from the general education curriculum or from the student's individualized education program (IEP). The key is to collaborate with the student's general education teacher to identify the goals and objectives to be addressed through EI and to balance academic and ecologically valid goals and objectives (e.g., functional/adaptive).

The second activity is to conduct a baseline probe of the student's performance on the goal or objective. The baseline probe establishes the student's level of performance prior to instruction so the effectiveness of the EI teaching plan can be evaluated. In addition, the information gathered during the baseline probe will be used to design the EI teaching plan so that it is tailored to the student's individual learning needs.

Finally, while preparing for instruction the teacher must develop a trial distribution schedule. This activity focuses on identifying opportunities to provide EI during ongoing classroom routines and activities (e.g., naturally occurring breaks in instruction). In addition, it allows the teacher to systematically plan the specific times and the number of EI trials presented to the student in an instructional session.

Step 2: Design an Embedded Instruction Program

The focus of this step is to structure the teaching plan to ensure that key components of the teaching interaction are clearly articulated prior to beginning EI.

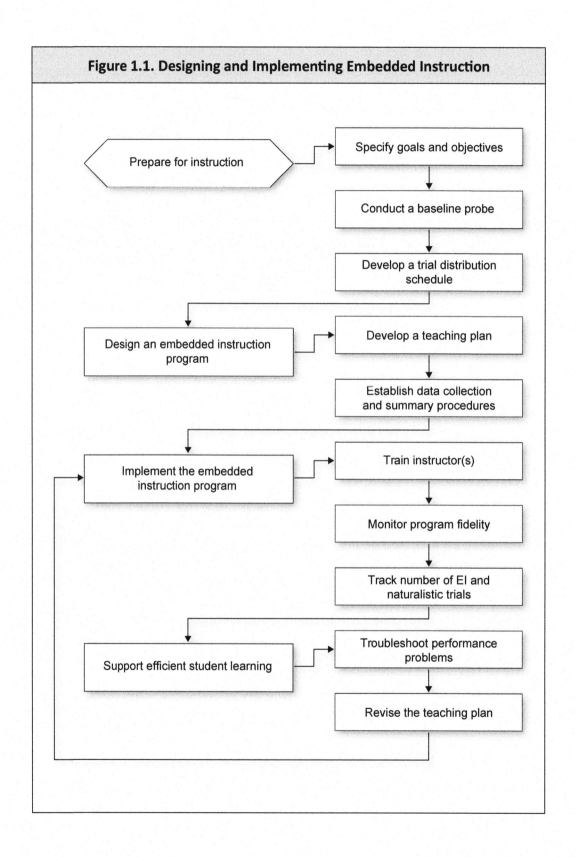

Figure 1.1. Designing and Implementing Embedded Instruction

These components include (a) the times at which instructional trials are presented to the student, (b) the specific instructional examples that are presented during the trials, (c) the response prompts provided to the student to ensure correct responding and the criterion for fading support, and (d) the steps for correcting student errors and reinforcing correct responses. The specificity of the teaching plan is critical in ensuring that EI is consistently delivered by all individuals who are serving as instructors (i.e. teachers, paraprofessionals, peers). In addition, the scripted nature of the teaching plan is intended to provide maximum procedural support to individuals who may not have experience in providing systematic instruction to individuals with IDD.

The second critical activity in this step is the development of data collection and summary procedures. The process uses regularly scheduled "probes" to assess student performance in the EI teaching plan without instructional support. This provides an independent and reliable means of assessing student progress and determining when and how to reduce the demands on instructors who are trying to implement EI within the ongoing routines and activities of the classroom.

Step 3: Implement the Program

The best teaching plan will only be effective if the individuals implementing the plan reliably follow the procedures laid out by the special education teacher. Consequently, effectively training instructors (i.e., general education teachers, paraprofessionals, peer tutors) to implement the teaching plan is vital. The long-term success of EI is enhanced if the special education teacher systematically monitors the correct implementation of the teaching plan. This activity involves regular observation of, and feedback to, instructors.

Finally, the teaching plan will only be successful if the student receives an adequate number of instructional trials each day. This can be determined either by the teacher during their regular observations of the instructors and evaluations of instruction data, or by asking instructors to track the number and type of instructional trials provided to the student during each lesson and making a data-based decision.

Step 4: Support Student Learning

No teaching plan is perfect. Teachers must regularly examine the student performance during probe sessions to determine whether changes in the teaching strategies are needed. This examination should focus on the specific errors that the student is making, in order to develop a hypothesis for why the student is making these errors and to revise the instruction program to respond to the errors.

Illustrating the Process

Each step and activity in this process can be more completely explained and illustrated through the use of vignettes. Here are two typical situations.

Jacob

Jacob is a 15-year-old ninth grader with moderate intellectual disability. Jacob communicates using two- to three-word sentences, with difficulty articulating some words. He attends his neighborhood junior high school and is enrolled in several general education classes during the day. One of the classes is a foods and nutrition class taken by ninth graders. Prior to his IEP meeting, Jacobs's special education teacher and his foods and nutrition teacher met to discuss specific goals and objectives for him in that class. The district curriculum for the class requires that all students be able to read, define, and apply a number of concepts in planning and preparing balanced and nutritious meals. Jacob's teachers identified several skills from the curriculum that would be appropriate for him, and which would enhance both his participation in the class and his ability to prepare meals at home.

One of the skills that they identified was to read words or symbols that he could use to follow recipes. Ultimately, his IEP team decided that this skill would be targeted as an objective for his participation in the foods and nutrition class. A second, related objective focused on his use of these words in completing simple recipes to prepare his own lunches.

Jacob is supported in the foods class by a special education paraprofessional who is available to work with the teacher to implement modifications and provide assistance to Jacob as necessary to complete class activities. The paraprofessional provides Jack with EI trials during natural opportunities in the instruction provided by the general education teacher. Supplemental instructional trials are presented between class activities and during the natural breaks in class activities. During each class period, the paraprofessional presents Jacob with a combination of (a) EI trials designed to systematically promote his acquisition of the skill; and (b) naturalistic trials in the context of general education activities, designed to support generalization of the skill to new materials and activities. Each of these processes are described in greater detail in subsequent chapters of this book.

Lisa

Lisa is an 8-year-old student in the second grade diagnosed with autism spectrum disorder. Although Lisa had been given the WISC-III, a valid IQ score could not be established. Lisa is described by her teachers as very pleasant but passive.

For example, she complies with verbal requests (when paired with gestures) but does not initiate communication bids even when she needs something. She interacts minimally with peers and only slightly more with specific adults. Lisa has demonstrated some verbal imitation (i.e., repeating single words) but does not use words to express her wants and needs. She also has a speech-generating device but did not use it to communicate with others in the environment. She receives occupational therapy services weekly and demonstrates some motor imitation. Lisa often has to be redirected to instructional tasks and needs lots of reinforcement to remain on task. She participates in the general education class during opening activities and language arts in the morning, and science and fine arts in the afternoon. Lisa is supported in the class by a special education paraprofessional who provides her with the response prompts, error correction, and social reinforcement as necessary to complete class activities.

Lisa's IEP team includes her parents, the special education teacher, the general education teacher, the speech and language pathologist, and the occupational therapist. The team has decided to make communication a primary focus of her IEP. In the past, Lisa's parents and teachers tried to teach her to communicate using single words, manual signs, and a picture exchange communication system. Although Lisa would imitate some words and signs, she did not use any of these methods to spontaneously communicate at home or at school. The team has decided to try an electronic communication device with vocal output. They used a person-centered planning approach to focus communication on specific things that might be important to Lisa. One of the objectives included in her IEP targets her use of the communication device to request help when needed help on a difficult task, or when unanticipated situations arise.

EI trials are provided by the paraprofessional assigned to support her in the general education class. EI trials on the use of her communication device are distributed throughout the day to help promote the generalized use of her device. The paraprofessional was trained to take advantage of all natural opportunities for Lisa to use her communication device. For example, when she needs assistance to complete a task the paraprofessional provides an EI trial. However, to ensure that Lisa has a sufficient number of opportunities to learn to use her device, the teacher and the paraprofessional engineer situations throughout the day to provide supplemental EI trials, such as asking Lisa to complete an assignment for which she does not have all the necessary materials.

Summary

Implementing EI requires a four-step process. In the first step, the teacher prepares for instruction by specifying goals, collecting baseline data, and developing a trial distribution schedule. In the second step, the teacher designs an EI program by formulating a teaching plan and establishing data collection procedures. In the third step, the teacher implements the EI program, training instructors, monitoring program fidelity, and tracking the number of trials. Finally, the teacher supports efficient student learning by making data-based decisions and revising the teaching plan as appropriate.

The following chapters are designed to illustrate how EI can be implemented with students with IDD in general education classes. Each chapter includes one or more forms developed to assist teachers to design and implement EI. Blanks of these forms are included in Appendix A.

CHAPTER 2

Preparing for Instruction

The development and implementation of effective embedded instruction (EI) requires teachers to complete several preparatory activities. These activities include (a) developing specific instruction goals and objectives for the student's participation in the general education class, (b) conducting baseline probes to assess the student's current performance of the target skills, and (c) developing a trial distribution schedule that allows teachers to target when instructional trials will be presented to the student.

Develop Specific Instruction Goals and Objectives

The first step in creating an effective education program is to develop instruction goals and objectives that explicitly define the expected outcomes for the student. In inclusive education programs, this means that the student's individualized education program (IEP) must include goals and objectives that clearly define what knowledge and skills should be demonstrated as a result of instruction in the general education class. If the expected education outcomes for the student are not clearly defined, it is possible for the student to be physically present in the classroom while functionally excluded from meaningful instruction (Schuster, Hemmeter, & Ault, 2001).

Hunt, Soto, Maier, and Doering (2003) described a process for developing unified plans of support (UPS). The focus of this process is to ensure that students' IEPs identify meaningful learning outcomes that are consistent with the general education curriculum, and with the routines and activities of the general education class. However, the UPS process goes beyond simply identifying meaningful learning outcomes; it includes the development of specific supports necessary to ensure that the IEP is implemented successfully. The UPS process comprises four key steps:

1. The team identifies the learning and social profile of the student.
2. Based on the profile, the team brainstorms curricular, instruction, and social support strategies that will allow the student to successfully participate in each domain of the general education curriculum.

3. Once each support strategy is identified, a team member is responsible for ensuring that the strategy is put into place and for coordinating the activities of other team members implementing the strategy.
4. The team develops and implements a system of accountability to evaluate the effectiveness of the UPS in meeting the student's needs. This involves regular team meetings to allow the team members to analyze the effect of each strategy and refine the UPS.

When utilizing this type of teaming process, EI would be considered one of many potential strategies for supporting effective student learning. As indicated by the UPS process, the responsibility for designing and implementing EI would be assigned to one team member. Typically, this would be the student's special education teacher, who would collaborate with the general education teacher, paraprofessionals, peers, and other staff members to ensure that the EI program was being implemented successfully. Finally, the team would regularly review the effectiveness of the EI teaching plan and refine it as necessary to ensure student success.

Some of the goals and objectives identified by the IEP team may focus on the student's acquisition of skills included in the typical general education curriculum. These objectives can be designed to focus on a subset of skills that are appropriate for the student, and target responses and evaluation procedures that will accommodate the student's unique education needs (Hunt, McDonnell, & Crockett, 2012). For example (as described in Chapter 1), Jacob's IEP team identified a goal of learning to read words and symbols from the general foods and nutrition curriculum that could be incorporated into recipes he would use at home.

In other cases, goals and objectives may focus on the student's unique education needs distinct from those in the typical general education curriculum. For example, Lisa's IEP team decided that she should learn how to request assistance from peers, staff, and teachers when encountering a difficult task during class routines and activities. Although this skill is not in the general education curriculum, the ability to request help from others improves her ability to function successfully in the general education class and other settings. Including both types of goals and objectives in the IEP—those within and those distinct from the general education curriculum—can provide students with an education program designed to meet their unique needs and promote their successful participation in school, home, and community settings.

The development of meaningful goals and objectives for general education classes requires collaboration. The premise of professionals working together to develop a student's IEP has been an essential principle of the Individuals With Disabilities Education Act (IDEA) since it was enacted. A substantial amount of literature suggests that developing and implementing IEPs that effectively support students' inclusion in general education classes requires a collaborative teaming process (Giangreco, Dennis, Cloninger, Edelman, & Schattman, 1993; Hunt, Doering, Hirose-Hatae, Maier, & Goetz, 2001; Hunt et al., 2003; Salisbury, Evans, & Palombaro, 1997; York-Barr, Schultz, Doyle, Kronberg, & Crossett, 1996).

Conduct a Baseline Probe

Prior to implementing EI, the teacher should conduct a baseline probe. The baseline probe has three purposes. First, the probe determines the student's level of performance before EI begins, in order to establish a basis for determining whether performance improves across instructional sessions. Second, the probe identifies how much (if any) of the targeted skill the student can already perform correctly and independently. Finally, the probe identifies the type of assistance that will be necessary to allow the student consistently to complete the target skill correctly. This information is used to identify the level of assistance needed to support student success.

Assess the Student's Performance

Baseline probes are used to determine how much of the target skill the student can already do and what he still needs to learn. Figure 2.1 presents an illustrative baseline probe form for Jacob. In this example, the baseline probe focused on whether he could read any of the cooking words and measurement symbols that had been selected for instruction. In the first column, the teacher listed the words and symbols selected for EI. The teacher assessed Jacob's performance by presenting a flash card with the word or symbol printed on it and presenting the cue "What does this say?" She coded Jacob's responses either correct (with a "+") or incorrect (with a "0") in the second column. Teachers should collect baseline data across several sessions in order to establish a stable pattern of performance and to ensure that the data accurately reflect student performance. The data in Jacob's probe shows that he was able to correctly read three words and symbols (i.e., *pan*, *ladle*, and *C*) across three baseline probe sessions. These three skills will be eliminated from the list of targeted skills when his teacher develops the EI teaching plan.

Figure 2.2 illustrates how Lisa's teacher and a paraprofessional used the same procedures to establish her baseline performance. The data indicate that she did not initiate pressing the Help icon during any of the probe trials. Based on the three baseline probes, Mrs. Wright and the paraprofessional decided that all of the situations assessed during the probe should be included in the EI teaching plan.

Figure 2.1. Jacob's Baseline Probe Form

Student: Jacob   Teacher: Ms. Smith

Instructional cue: "What does this say?"

Example	1/5		1/6		1/7	
	+/0	Prompt	+/0	Prompt	+/0	Prompt
Pan	+		+		+	
Casserole	0	M	0	M	0	M
Colander	0	M	0	M	0	M
Ladle	+		+		+	
Spoon	0	M	0	M	0	M
Tongs	0	M	0	M	0	M
Spatula	0	M	0	M	0	M
Whisk	0	M	0	M	0	M
Strainer	0	M	0	M	0	M
Tsp	0	M	0	M	0	M
Tbsp	0	M	0	M	0	M
C	+		+		+	
Qt	0	M	0	M	0	M
Oz	0	M	0	M	0	M
Lb	0	M	0	M	0	M
% Correct	20%		20%		20%	

Prompt Key: V – Verbal   M – Model   G – Gesture/Point   P – Prime   F – Full Physical

Figure 2.2. Lisa's Baseline Probe Form

Student: Lisa **Teacher:** Mrs. Wright **Paraprofessional:** Ms. Petty

Instructional cue: "What do you want?"

Example	Instructor	10/16		10/17		10/18	
		+/0	Prompt	+/0	Prompt	+/0	Prompt
Difficult discrimination	MW	0	G	0	F	0	G
Difficult motor response	SP	0	G	0	F	0	F
Incorrect materials	SP	0	V	0	G	0	V
Unclear directions or instructions	MW	0	V	0	V	0	V
% Correct		0		0		0	

Prompt Key: V – Verbal   M – Model   G – Gesture/Point   P – Prime   F – Full physical

Identify the Level of Assistance

Another critical purpose of the baseline probe is to determine the amount of assistance that the student requires to consistently complete the correct response during instruction. This can be accomplished by implementing a prompting system known as the *system of least prompts* (see Chapter 3) each time the student makes an error during the probe.

When using a system of least prompts, the teacher systematically provides increasing levels of assistance to the student until he makes the correct response. The type of prompts provided to the student range from verbal directions to hand-over-hand physical assistance and are selected based on the skill that is being taught. The teacher conducts baseline probes until the prompt that consistently results in the correct response is identified and documented on the data sheet. For example, Jacob did not respond when his teacher presented the flash card with the word *casserole* printed on it. After presenting the cue ("What does this say?"), she waited for several seconds and then said "casserole," and Jacob repeated the word. If Jacob had not imitated her model, she would have provided a more explicit verbal prompt to Jacob to say the word after she did (i.e., "Jacob, this word says *casserole*. Say *casserole*."). After the probe trial, Ms. Smith entered an M in the third column of the form to record the level of assistance he needed (modeling) to read the word correctly. This information is used to design the assistance strategy for Jacob's EI program.

In contrast, Lisa required a number of different prompts— ranging from verbal prompts to full physical—to press the Help icon on her communication device. This information will need to be taken into consideration in selecting the type of response prompting and fading procedure to be used, and in designing the procedure so that it ensures Lisa's correct responding during instruction.

Develop a Trial Distribution Schedule

A key difference between EI and traditional instructional approaches is that in EI the instructional trials are distributed within and across classroom activities. There are three critical steps in developing an effective EI schedule.

Identify the Number of Instructional Trials

The rate at which students learn new skills is directly linked to the number of instructional trials they receive (Brophy & Good, 1986; Clark, Haydon, Bauer, & Epperly, 2016; Collins, 2012; Greenwood, Delquadri, & Hall, 1984; Reynolds, 1991; Rosenshine & Stevens, 1986). Put simply, the more opportunities students have to practice a skill, the faster they will learn it. The initial number of instructional trials to present to a student within a given program is a professionally subjective judgment based on (a) the student's functioning level, (b) the complexity of the skill being taught, and (c) the structure of the activities and routines of the general education class. A reasonable measure of how many trials the student will need is the student's previous learning history with similar skills and in similar situations. In general, it is probably better to overestimate the number of trials that the student will need rather than underestimate.

Jacob's teacher decided that he should receive at least five presentations of each word or symbol name each day. This meant that she would need to identify at least five situations during the foods class when the paraprofessional could present the words or symbols without disrupting the class or interfering with Jacob's involvement in other class activities.

Determine How Trials Should be Distributed

Once the number of instructional trials necessary to promote learning is identified, the teacher must decide whether the trials will be presented within a single class period or across class periods throughout the school day. For example, teaching Jacob to read vocabulary words in the foods class would most logically be done within the regularly scheduled foods class period. In Lisa's case, skills might be more effectively taught throughout the day. That is, in teaching Lisa to request assistance, it would be more effective to distribute instructional trials throughout the day because she will need to use this skill across areas of the curriculum and in different activities.

Estimate the Frequency of Teaching Opportunities

When determining the frequency of teaching opportunities, teachers should consider how to incorporate both natural and supplemental embedded instruction trials in teaching opportunities. Natural embedded instruction trials are not directly controlled by the teacher and present themselves periodically to the student within the normal flow of instructional activities presented by the general education teacher. Natural instructional trials have both advantages and disadvantages. A significant advantage is that they create opportunities for the student to respond to typical materials and in typical situations. This increases the likelihood that the student will develop a generalized skill that can be used in new contexts and situations. For example, natural embedded instruction trials could occur as a result of students interacting with materials. In Jacob's foods class, it is likely that there will be opportunities for him to read the targeted words and symbols on worksheets or in the textbook. Natural instructional trials also can be linked to specific instructional activities presented by the teacher.

In Jacob's case, there might be opportunities for him to read the target words and symbols while completing a recipe during a cooking lab or while putting cooking utensils away following a teacher demonstration. The disadvantage of natural instructional trials is that the teacher might not always be able to predict when these instructional trials will occur. This may reduce the potential effectiveness of instruction because the teacher may not be able to provide a consistent number of trials to the student.

To ensure that the instruction will be successful, the teacher can provide supplemental EI trials to the student. Supplemental trials are directly controlled by the individual implementing the program. They are planned teaching opportunities that occur at specific times within or across class periods. In many respects, supplemental EI trials look and feel much like the discrete trials presented to students during traditional one-to-one or small-group instruction formats. Previous research suggests that there are several common situations in general education classes in which supplemental trials can be presented (Johnson & McDonnell, 2004; Johnson, McDonnell, Holzwarth, & Hunter, 2004; McDonnell, Johnson, Polychronis, & Riesen, 2002; Wolery, Anthony, Snyder, Werts, & Katzenmeyer, 1997).

One possibility for supplemental trials in EI uses the transitions between instructional activities. For example, an instructional trial could be presented to a student as the class moves from a group instructional activity to independent seat work. Another common opportunity is natural breaks in activities; in the foods class, for example, there may be some "down time" when students are waiting for food to come out of the oven during the cooking lab. Finally, EI might be provided when students are working independently at their desks.

Appendix A includes a Trial Distribution Planning Form that teachers can use to determine the number of teaching opportunities that are available to teach a skill to a student. The first step is to list the potential natural and supplemental teaching opportunities. Once these teaching opportunities have been identified, the teacher should list the classes, activities, or routines in which the skill will be taught. The form allows teachers to enter up to five different settings or contexts. Next, the teacher should develop an estimate of the frequency of teaching opportunities that will occur in each class period or activity. Once this information is entered, the teacher can calculate the total number of instructional opportunities that will be available to teach the skill to the student each day.

As illustrated in Figure 2.3, Jacob's teacher focused her analysis on both the natural and the supplemental instructional trials typically available during the foods class. In completing the form, she first estimated the number of natural EI trials that might be available during a class period. These estimates were based on her discussions with the general education teacher and her prior observations of the class. Next, she estimated the frequency of the potential supplemental embedded instruction trials. Her analysis suggested that typically there would be an opportunity to present between 12 and 25 natural and supplemental instruction trials to Jacob each day. Because she had previously determined Jacob's instructional need to be five trials per target, she concluded that EI could be used to effectively teach Jacob to read the words and symbols without providing him with additional one-to-one or small-group instruction.

Figure 2.3. Trial Distribution Planning Form for Jacob

Student: Jacob		Teacher: Ms. Smith				
Potential teaching opportunities		Class/Activity/Routine				Total opportunities
		Foods class				
Supplemental instructional trials	Activity transitions (opening to lecture; lecture to individual or group activities; going to lab)	3				3
	Natural breaks in activities (lab)	1-3				1-3
	Management tasks (roll; distribution of graded assignments)	1-2				1-2
	Independent work	3-6				3-6
Natural instructional trials	Vocabulary worksheets	1-3				1-3
	Lab planner	1-3				1-3
	Recipes	1				1
	Text	1-5				1-5
	Potential opportunities	12-25				12-25

Lisa's teacher concluded that natural opportunities for requesting help in the second-grade class would occur at a relatively low rate during the day, based on her discussion with the general education teacher and her observations of the classroom (see Figure 2.4). It became clear that supplemental instructional trials would need to be engineered to provide more opportunities for Lisa to learn when to request help. Mrs. Wright identified times during the typical routines and activities of the class in which these trials could be presented without disrupting the other students and the general education teacher.

Figure 2.4. Trial Distribution Planning Form for Lisa

Student: Jacob **Teacher:** Ms. Wright

	Potential teaching opportunities	Class/Activity/Routine					Total opportunities
		Opening	Language arts	Science	Fine arts		
Supplemental instructional trials	Activity transitions (opening to lecture; lecture to individual or group activities; going to lab)	1	1	1	1		4
	Natural breaks in activities (lab)	1	1	1	1		4
	Management tasks (roll; distribution of graded assignments)	1	1	1	1		4
	Independent work	1-2	1-2	1-2	0		4-8
Natural instructional trials	Text	1	1	1	0		3
	Worksheets	1	1	1	0		3
	Collaborative group activities and projects	1	1	1	1		4
	Large group discussions	1	1	1	1		4
	Potential opportunities	8-10	8-10	8-10	4		28-34

Summary

In preparing to implement EI, the student's IEP team must collaborate to identify learning goals and objectives so the student can meaningfully participate in the general education class. Once EI has been selected as an instructional strategy, the teacher should conduct a baseline probe in order to establish the student's entry level of performance on the target skills. The baseline probe also provides important information to the teacher about the examples and response prompts that should be included in the teaching plan. Finally, to promote efficient learning, the teacher should identify opportunities for natural and supplemental embedded instructional trials within the ongoing classroom routines and activities.

CHAPTER 3

Designing an Embedded Instruction Program

The basic elements of an embedded instruction (EI) program are similar to those used in traditional special education classes. Prior to implementing an EI program, the teacher should prepare a teaching plan and develop data collection procedures for ongoing assessment of the student's performance.

Write a Teaching Plan

Appendix A includes a form that teachers can use to write an EI teaching plan. To begin the process, the teacher should identify the instruction objective, and list the natural and supplemental teaching opportunities from the Trial Distribution Planning Form; Figure 3.1 illustrates how Jacob's and Lisa's teachers completed this initial planning. This information will serve as a reminder to the individuals implementing the program about the expected outcomes of EI and when instructional trials may be delivered to the student. The process of developing an EI teaching plan includes four additional steps: (a) selecting instructional examples and developing teaching materials, (b) sequencing instructional examples, (c) developing assistance strategies, and (d) developing reinforcement and error-correction procedures.

Identify Performance Contexts and Develop Teaching Materials

Research consistently suggests that many students with intellectual and developmental disabilities (IDD) have difficulty generalizing skills learned in one context or setting to new contexts or settings (Horner, McDonnell, & Bellamy, 1986; McDonnell et al., In press; Rosenthal-Malek & Bloom, 1998). For example, a student might use signs to request desired items at school with his teacher but not be able to use the signs at home with his parents. Another student may learn to use one type of calculator to complete single-digit addition problems but not be able to do the same problems with a different calculator. Effectively addressing this problem requires that the teacher develop a teaching plan designed to promote generalized responding—from the very beginning. This is accomplished by identifying the full range of situations and settings across which the student

Figure 3.1. Developing the Embedded Instruction Teaching Plan

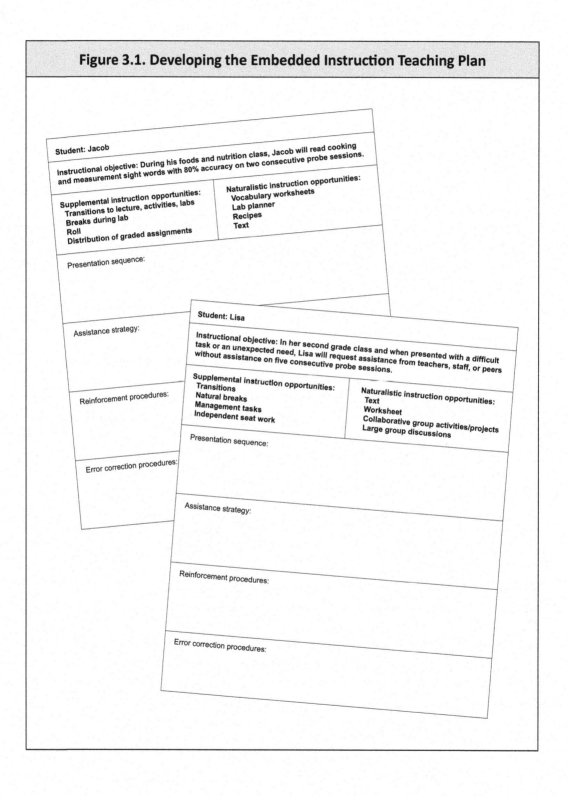

must use the skill, and then developing instructional examples and materials that systematically present the necessary situational variations to the student across trials and sessions (McDonnell & Ferguson, 1988). To accomplish this, the teacher should (a) identify the performance contexts in which the student will use the skill, (b) identify how these performance contexts are different from each other, and (c) identify and develop instructional examples and materials that represent the range of variation across likely performance contexts.

Identify the performance contexts in which the student will use the skill. The teacher must first decide where and when the student will be required to use the skill. For example, in Jacob's case, he should be able to read the target words and symbols during instructional activities in his foods class and when completing recipes at home. For Lisa, the variation in requesting help is related more to specific situations in which she should ask for assistance rather than settings. This information will help their teachers identify the range of situations that the students will encounter in using the skill from day to day, and how their use of the targeted skill will change based on this variation.

Identify how the performance contexts are different from each other. Once the range of performance contexts has been identified, the teacher should identify the ways that these contexts differ from each other. For the target words and symbols presented to Jacob, one of the biggest differences is the physical characteristics of the words. For instance, the size of the letters, the font, and the color of the letters in the word *whisk* will vary based on whether he is reading from a textbook, from a worksheet developed by the teacher, or from a recipe in a cookbook. For Lisa, determining when to request help will vary significantly across different situations and requires her to recognize that she either does not know what to do or that she does not have the necessary materials to complete a task. This information helps the teacher determine the kinds of supplemental instructional examples that should be presented to the student across teaching sessions and how the instructional materials will need to be designed to ensure that the student develops a generalized response.

Develop instructional examples and materials that expose students to variations in performance contexts. When teaching generalized responses, teachers need to present examples and materials to students that require them to respond correctly across the variations found in the intended performance contexts. In EI programs, this can be accomplished by designing teaching examples and materials that vary across EI trials. It is also accomplished by identifying opportunities within the ongoing activities of the general education class to present naturalistic instruction trials. In Jacob's case, Ms. Smith needed teaching materials for EI trials that reflected the different physical characteristics of the target words and symbols Jacob would encounter. She developed a set of flash cards that varied the size, font, and color of each of his target words (see Figure 3.2) and which could be presented to Jacob across EI trials within a class period. Ideally, Jacob would never see the same flash card twice in a class period.

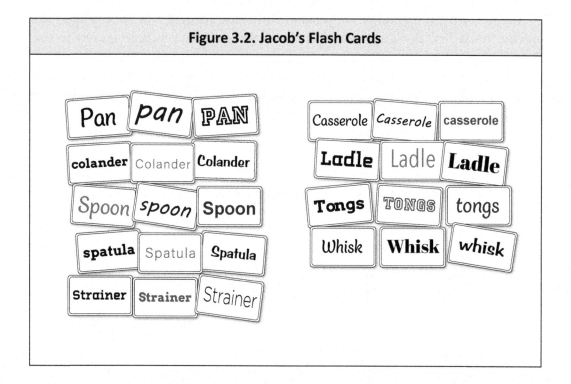

Figure 3.2. Jacob's Flash Cards

Mrs. Wright decided that teaching generalized responses could be accomplished by presenting Lisa with different situations (e.g., pointing to the correct word during language arts, using scissors during fine arts) within and across class periods. Mrs. Wright and Lisa's paraprofessional will need to engineer different examples within each "help" category (e.g., difficult discriminations, difficult motor responses) each day. Their goal will be to present as many different examples within each "help" category as possible across the week.

Development of generalized responses is also promoted by taking advantage of the natural teaching opportunities that are presented during the ongoing activities of the class. For example, this could be accomplished by asking Jacob to read the word *whisk* each time it is presented on a worksheet, in the textbook, in a recipe, and so on. The physical characteristics of the word *whisk*—as well as whether it is presented in isolation, in a sentence, or as label for a picture—are likely to vary substantially across each of these contexts. For Lisa, her paraprofessional would look for situations in which Lisa was not successfully completing a task assigned to other students in the class, and prompt her to ask for help from her peers or teacher.

Develop a Presentation Sequence

Developing an effective example presentation sequence requires the teacher to determine how many instructional examples should be presented to the student at one time. The teacher then arranges the sequence so examples can be cumulatively introduced to the student across instructional sessions.

How many instructional examples can be presented to the student at one time? A key decision in developing a teaching plan is deciding how many examples can be introduced to the student at one time. Systematically controlling the introduction and presentation of examples can significantly increase the efficiency of instruction and reduce the number of errors that the student makes while learning the skill. Because it would probably be too difficult for Jacob to learn all of the words and symbols simultaneously, Ms. Smith needs to divide the complete list of targeted words into smaller teaching sets and introduce them in a way that allows him to retain the skill across time. Jacob's baseline probe (see Chapter 2) indicated that he could only read three of the 15 words and symbols that were selected for instruction. Ms. Smith decided that she would break the remaining 12 words into three teaching sets, each consisting of four words or symbols.

By dividing examples into sets, teachers can both control the difficulty of the instructional task for students and increase the speed at which they learn a skill. Deciding how many examples can be presented to a student is based on several factors:

- *The student's previous learning history.* A fundamental principle of effective instruction is that strategies are tailored to a student's specific needs. The best basis on which to make a decision about how many examples to include in a teaching set is the student's previous performance in other instructional programs.

- *The complexity or difficulty of the skill.* The size of the teaching set should also be based on the complexity or difficulty of the skill being taught. The goal is to present the maximum number of examples that allow the student to experience success. As a result, more complex or difficult skills will probably require the teacher to develop smaller teaching sets.

- *The nature of the teaching opportunities.* Another consideration involves the characteristics of the teaching opportunities available within class periods or activities. For example, Jacob's teachers might have less time to present instructional examples during transitions between instructional activities (e.g., between small-group discussion and starting work on a worksheet) in the foods class than during independent work at the lab station.

How will teaching examples be sequenced? *Cumulative sequencing* is an especially effective strategy for introducing a large number of teaching examples to students. In this strategy, the first teaching example is introduced and taught to criterion. Then, the second example is introduced and taught to criterion. In the third step of the sequence, the student is required to accurately respond to both examples when presented randomly. Each subsequent teaching example initially is taught by itself, then all of the previously taught examples are mixed together and presented randomly to the student. This strategy allows teachers to cumulatively increase the number of examples students complete, and provides students with regular opportunities to review previously taught examples.

This strategy can be applied to individual teaching examples or to sets of examples. Figure 3.3 presents the sequences developed by Jacob's and Lisa's teachers. In Jacob's case, Ms. Smith plans to introduce the first four vocabulary words to Jacob and provide instruction until he can read the words at the expected criterion. Then, she will introduce the second set of words and teach it to criterion. In the third step of the sequence, Ms. Smith will ask Jacob to read all of the words in the first two sets when they are presented randomly during the class session. This ensures that Jacob is not mixing up words that are similar in structure (i.e., *spatula* and *spoon*) and that he has not forgotten the first four words that were taught. In the fourth step of the sequence, Ms. Smith will teach the next set of words and then, finally, he will be required to read all 12 words and symbols when presented in random order throughout the class session.

Lisa's teacher decided to use a different approach to teach her to request help. Instead of cumulatively introducing the "help" categories to her, Mrs. Wright decided to randomly present different examples within each category throughout the day. This procedure is called *concurrent presentation*. Mrs. Wright selected this procedure because (a) it would be difficult, if not impossible, to present multiple embedded instruction trials at one time to Lisa; and (b) there was only one possible response that Lisa could make (i.e., press the Help icon) to each example that was presented. In these cases, the random presentation of examples allows the student to be exposed to the full range of variation associated with the target skill and to learn a generalized response.

Select and Use Teaching Procedures That Support Generalization

The ability to generalize the performance of previously mastered skills across time (i.e., *skill maintenance*) is critical to the success of students with IDD in home,

Chapter 3

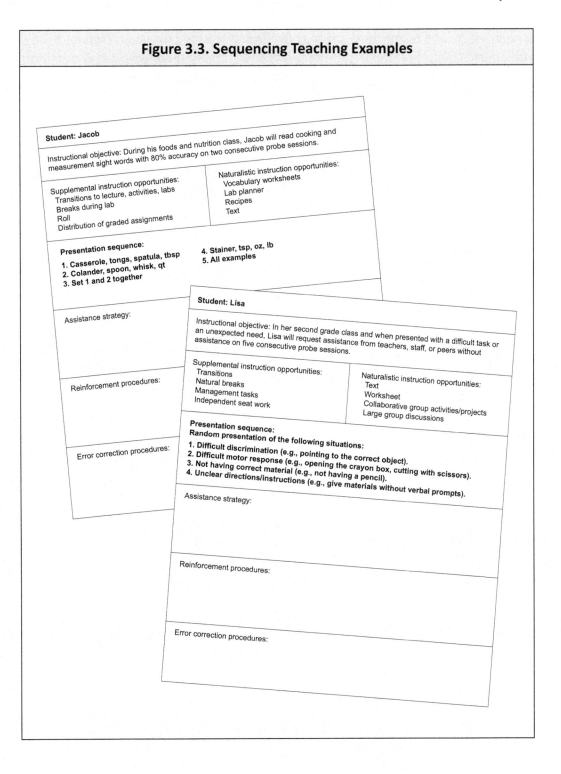

Figure 3.3. Sequencing Teaching Examples

school, work, and community settings (McDonnell, et al., In press; Wolery, Bailey, and Sugai, 1988). Maintenance—generalization across time—can be understood as the phase of learning where an individual consistently performs a skill, trained to criterion, independently over time with only naturally occurring reinforcing consequences. This is especially important because many student-acquired skills are prerequisites for learning more complex skills and tasks. For example, a secondary student with IDD must maintain fluent math and calculator skills to be able to balance a weekly budget. Although there is little research on methods to promote skill maintenance, we recommend teaching programs focus on four critical procedural aspects:

- Select a rigorous criterion for completion (e.g., 10 consecutive training sessions at 100% with no response prompts), because skill fluency has a direct impact on skill maintenance (Singer-Dudek & Greer, 2005).
- Provide regular opportunities to perform the skill after training. There is evidence that, without opportunities to respond, there will be significant reductions in the rates of skill maintenance (Collins, 2012; Horner, Williams, & Knobbe, 1985).
- Change reinforcement schedules through a systematic and successive shift from continuous to intermittent schedules of reinforcement until the skill is maintained under natural communities of reinforcement (Wolery et al., 1988).
- Use the generalization procedures previously described to ensure the behavior will be maintained across relevant settings, people, and stimulus variations.

By using these procedures during and after acquisition training, there is a greater likelihood that the skill will be maintained.

Develop an Assistance Strategy

Most students with IDD will need assistance from a teacher to learn new skills. A variety of prompting strategies can be used, including providing physical assistance (e.g., hand-over-hand to help the student write the letters of his first name), picture prompts (e.g., providing the student with a printed card of his name so that she can copy her name onto her worksheet), modeling (e.g., demonstrating how the letters of his first name are made), and verbal directions (e.g., telling the student to print her first name in the upper-right-hand corner). After students begin to acquire a skill, teachers should begin to fade prompts so that students ultimately can perform the skill without assistance.

Research has validated a number of fading strategies with students with IDD (McDonnell, Snell, Brown, Coleman, & Eichelberger, 2019): the system of most prompts, time delay, graduated guidance, and the system of least prompts. Although all of these strategies can be used to teach new skills, we recommend that teachers use a **constant time-delay strategy** for most students and skills. A number of studies have shown that constant time-delay is an effective strategy for students with IDD, including those in EI programs (Johnson & McDonnell, 2004; McDonnell et al., 2002; Riesen, McDonnell, Johnson, Polychronis, & Jameson, 2003). In addition, teachers and paraprofessionals participating in these studies have reported that constant time delay is a simple and easy strategy to implement within the ongoing routines and activities of general education classes.

In the constant time-delay procedure, the teacher initiates an instructional trial by presenting the example and a cue so that the student knows what is expected. The teacher then provides a *controlling prompt*, which is the form of assistance that is the least intrusive necessary to ensure that the student correctly completes the expected response. In the first step of constant time delay, the teacher presents the controlling prompt to the student immediately following the example and the instructional cue. This step is referred to as the *0-second delay* step. The teacher continues to implement this step until the student responds consistently to the prompt.

In the second step, the teacher delays the presentation of the controlling prompt for a fixed time interval. Typically, this delay is several seconds. Delaying the controlling prompt provides the student an opportunity to respond correctly without help or additional information. If the student doesn't correctly complete the response during the delay period, then the teacher provides the controlling prompt to the student.

Successfully implementing constant time-delay within an EI program requires teachers to identify a cue that will tell the student what he is expected to do, identify the controlling prompt, and determine how long the delay period should be.

Identify an instructional cue. Often the instructional cue can be a verbal direction that tells the student that it is time to respond and what he is to do. However, many types of assistance could be used as an instructional cue. Instructional cues should be selected based on student preference, the nature of the skill, and the expected response.

Identify the controlling prompt. Research suggests that teachers should attempt to minimize the number of errors that students make when they are first learning a new skill (Collins, 2012; McDonnell et al., in press). This in turn minimizes the need for students to subsequently "unlearn" their mistakes. Teachers should use controlling prompts that are most likely to result in students making the correct response during each instructional trial. Information obtained during the baseline probe helps the teacher in this part of the process. During the baseline probe, the teacher should identify the type and amount of assistance necessary for the student to correctly complete the desired response. This assistance strategy is then used as the controlling prompt in both steps of the constant time-delay procedure.

Determine the length of the delay period. There are no validated rules for selecting the length for the delay period in a constant time-delay procedure. The delay periods in research studies examining constant time delay have varied widely (Collins, 2012). A teacher's decision about the length of the delay period will always be somewhat subjective. One approach to help make this process more systematic is to estimate—or literally test, with some willing volunteers—how quickly students without disabilities would typically respond in similar situations. Once this has been established, the teacher can adjust the delay period to accommodate the unique characteristics and needs of the student. Three-second to 10-second delays are typical.

Figure 3.4 presents the constant time-delay procedure developed by Jacob's teacher. In the first step, each instructional trial begins with the Ms. Smith presenting a flash card (e.g., *tsp* for *teaspoon*) and providing the instructional cue "What does this say?"—immediately providing the controlling prompt by saying "teaspoon." Instruction continues at this step until Jacob reliably responds correctly for each word in the teaching set.

In the second step of the procedure, Ms. Smith begins each trial by presenting a flash card and the instructional cue. However, instead of providing the controlling prompt immediately, she delays the modeling prompt for 3 seconds. If Jacob does not correctly read the word or symbol during the 3-second delay period, she presents the controlling prompt by saying "teaspoon."

In Lisa's case, her teacher previously had used constant time delay to teach several discrete skills with limited success. However, the system of least prompts had been effective in teaching her a variety of skills. Based on Lisa's previous learning history Mrs. Wright decided to use the system of least prompts to teach her to request help. Figure 3.5 illustrates how this system was entered on the teaching plan form.

Develop Reinforcement and Error-Correction Procedures

The last two components of the teaching plan are the reinforcement and error-correction procedures. Students can make three possible responses during an instructional trial when using a constant time-delay procedure: (a) correct responses that are not prompted by the teacher, (b) correct responses that are prompted by the teacher, and (c) incorrect responses (including no response). Teachers should develop specific consequence procedures to address each of these responses (Wolery, Ault, & Doyle, 1992). Once the teacher has developed procedures for each of these three possible responses, that information should be entered on the teaching plan.

Figure 3.4. Assistance Strategy for Jacob

Student: Jacob

Instructional objective:
During his foods and nutrition class, Jacob will read cooking and measurement sight words with 80% accuracy on two consecutive probe sessions.

Supplemental instruction opportunities:	Naturalistic instruction opportunities:
Transitions to lecture, activities, labs	Vocabulary worksheets
Breaks during lab	Lab planner
Roll	Recipes
Distribution of graded assignments	Text

Presentation sequence:
1. Casserole, tongs, spatula, tbsp
2. Colander, spoon, whisk, qt
3. Set 1 and 2 together
4. Strainer, tsp, oz, lb
5. All examples

Assistance strategy:
1. "What does this say?" present model immediately.
2. "What does this say?" delay model for 3 seconds.

Reinforcement procedures:

Error correction procedures:

Unprompted correct responses. An unprompted correct response means that the student makes the correct response before the teacher presents the controlling prompt. This response is exactly what the EI program is designed to establish. Consequently, the teacher should provide high levels of reinforcement for this response. For example, Jacob's teacher decided to provide descriptive social praise each time he read a word or symbol without any assistance. If he read the word before Ms. Smith could model it for him, she would say something like "Very good! That says [word/symbol name]."

Figure 3.5. Assistance Strategy for Lisa

Student: Lisa

Instructional objective:
In second grade class and when presented with a difficult task or an unexpected need, Lisa will request assistance from teachers, staff, or peers without assistance on five consecutive probe sessions.

Supplemental instruction opportunities:	Naturalistic instruction opportunities:
Transitions	Text
Natural breaks	Worksheet
Management tasks	Collaborative group activities/projects
Independent seat work	Large group discussions

Presentation sequence:
Random presentation of the following situations:
1. Difficult discrimination (e.g., pointing to the correct object).
2. Difficult motor response (e.g., opening the crayon box, cutting with scissors).
3. Not having correct material (e.g., not having a pencil).
4. Unclear directions/instructions (e.g., give materials without verbal prompts).

Assistance strategy (system of least prompts):
1. Situation presented—wait 3 sections.
2. Say "what do you want?" and point to communicator—wait 3 seconds.
3. Say "what do you want?" and point to the Help icon—wait 3 seconds.
4. Say "what do you want?" and provide physical assistance to touch Help icon.

Reinforcement procedures:

Error correction procedures:

Prompted correct responses. A prompted correct response means that the student makes the correct response after the controlling prompt has been presented by the teacher. In these instances, the teacher should confirm that the student made the correct response. However, the student should not be provided the same level of reinforcement as an unprompted independent correct response. This differential level of feedback is necessary to minimize the likelihood that the student will learn to wait for the teacher's prompt. For example, Ms. Smith decided to simply say "That says [word/symbol name)]" if he read the word or symbol correctly after her model.

Incorrect responses. The constant time-delay procedure is designed to minimize the number of incorrect responses that students make during instruction. (For these purposes, "no response" is considered to be an incorrect response.) Some degree of student error is unavoidable, however, and research suggests that the effectiveness of instruction can be improved if student errors are systematically corrected (Barbetta, Heron, & Heward, 1993; Barbetta, Heward, Bradley, & Miller, 1994). Teachers should use a four-step process to correct student errors:

1. Stop the instructional trial immediately and provide the student with feedback that he has made an incorrect response.
2. Present the example and instructional cue to the student.
3. Provide the student with the level of assistance necessary to ensure a correct response on the next attempt.
4. Provide feedback to confirm the correct response.

Finally, teachers should develop rules to guide systematically fading or increasing the level of support based on student performance. For example, a teacher may decide to use a most-to-least controlling prompt strategy, using baseline data to identify the level of controlling prompt needed to ensure errorless learning at each step of the instructional program. The teacher can then establish rules for systematically fading instructional support. For example,

> After 3 consecutive correct responses to a specified controlling prompt, the instructor will move to the next less-intrusive prompt in the hierarchy. After 2 errors using a specified controlling prompt, the instructor will move back to the previously used more intrusive prompt.

This sample procedure is simple and can be implemented quickly with a student. It also can be adapted for a wide variety of instructional tasks and skills. The error-correction procedure that Jacob's teacher plans to use with him based on this four-step procedure is presented in Figure 3.6.

Variations in reinforcement and error-correction procedures. The guidelines described here are equally applicable for reinforcing correct responses or correcting errors when using the simultaneous-prompting procedure, the system of most prompts, or the system of least prompts. However, teachers may need to provide additional information in the teaching plan about the prompt to be used to correct an error when using the system of most prompts or the system of least prompts. Figure 3.7 illustrates the reinforcement and error-correction procedures developed by Lisa's teacher for the system of least prompts.

Figure 3.6. Reinforcement and Error-Correction Procedures for Jacob

Student: Jacob

Instructional objective:
During his foods and nutrition class, Jacob will read cooking and measurement sight words with 80% accuracy on two consecutive probe sessions.

Supplemental instruction opportunities:	Naturalistic instruction opportunities:
Transitions to lecture, activities, labs Breaks during lab Roll Distribution of graded assignments	Vocabulary worksheets Lab planner Recipes Text

Presentation sequence:
1. Casserole, tongs, spatula, tbsp
2. Colander, spoon, whisk, qt
3. Set 1 and 2 together
4. Strainer, tsp, oz, lb
5. All examples

Assistance strategy:
1. "What does this say?" present model immediately.
2. "What does this say?" delay model for 3 seconds.

Reinforcement procedures:
Unprompted: Social praise plus "That says *word/symbol name*."
Prompted: "That says *word/symbol name*."

Error correction procedures:
Stop the trial immediately. Say "No, that's not right."
Represent the flash card and the cue "What does this say?"
Immediately provide a model of the work/symbol name.
Confirm the correct response by saying "That word says *word/symbol name*."

Establish Data Collection and Summary Procedures

Research has documented that the efficiency of instruction is improved if the teacher continuously tracks the student's performance (Collins, 2012; Farlow & Snell, 1994). This information can be used to help make timely modifications in the teaching procedures so that they can be tailored to the student's unique needs. General guidelines for carrying out data collection and interpreting student performance data have been discussed extensively elsewhere (Farlow

Chapter 3

> **Figure 3.7. Reinforcement and Error-Correction Procedures for Lisa**
>
> **Student: Lisa**
>
> Instructional objective:
> In second grade class and when presented with a difficult task or an unexpected need, Lisa will request assistance from teachers, staff, or peers without assistance on five consecutive probe sessions.
>
> | Supplemental instruction opportunities: | Naturalistic instruction opportunities: |
> |---|---|
> | Transitions | Text |
> | Natural breaks | Worksheet |
> | Management tasks | Collaborative group activities/projects |
> | Independent seat work | Large group discussions |
>
> Presentation sequence:
> Random presentation of the following situations:
> 1. Difficult discrimination (e.g., pointing to the correct object).
> 2. Difficult motor response (e.g., opening the crayon box, cutting with scissors).
> 3. Not having correct material (e.g., not having a pencil).
> 4. Unclear directions/instructions (e.g., give materials without verbal prompts).
>
> Assistance strategy (system of least prompts):
> 1. Situation presented—wait 3 sections.
> 2. Say "what do you want?" and point to communicator—wait 3 seconds.
> 3. Say "what do you want?" and point to the Help icon—wait 3 seconds.
> 4. Say "what do you want?" and provide physical assistance to touch Help icon.
>
> **Reinforcement procedures:**
> **Unprompted:** Provide descriptive social praise (e.g., "Excellent, you asked for help").
> **Prompted:** Provide feedback (e.g., "That's how you ask for help").
>
> **Error correction procedures:**
> Stop the trial immediately. Say "No, you need to ask for help."
> Immediately provide the next level of prompt in the sequence.
> Confirm the correct response by saying "That's how you ask for help."

& Snell, 1994; Westling & Fox, 2004; Wolery et al., 1988). Although continuous trial-by-trial data collection is a very common approach to gathering performance data with students with developmental disabilities, these procedures may be difficult to implement when instruction trials are distributed within and across activities in general education classes. Consequently, we recommend that teachers use data collection systems that are designed to regularly probe the student's performance of the target task.

In a **probe system**, the teacher probes or tests the student's performance of the skill on a fixed schedule. The decision about when probes should be conducted is based on factors such as the student's individual learning needs (e.g. communication needs, motor skill needs, social and emotional needs), the complexity of the task, the student's previous learning history, and the organization of the general education class. In the majority of the EI research studies conducted, acquisition data were collected 4 days a week and probe data (i.e., return to baseline condition) were collected once a week.

In Jacob's case, Ms. Smith decided that she should collect probe data on his performance twice a week. The probes were conducted by the paraprofessional during independent work periods scheduled by the general education teacher (see Figure 3.8). On January 9, the paraprofessional started conducting probes with Jacob on the words and symbols included in the first set. During each probe, she presented the flash cards in random order and asked, "What does this say?" She did not provide a model of the word during the probe. When Jacob read the word correctly, she entered a "+" on the probe sheet; she entered a "0" if he read it incorrectly. For example, the January 9 data indicate that Jacob was only able to read Tbsp., the symbol for tablespoon, correctly.

Figure 3.8. Data Collection Sheet for Jacob

Student: Jacob **Teacher: Ms. Smith**

Criterion for prompt changes: After 3 consecutive + move to less intrusive prompt
After 2 consecutive − move to a more intrusive prompt

Example/Item	Date					Skill maintenance probes				
	1/9	1/11	1/16	1/18	1/22					
Casserole	0	0	0	+	+					
Tongs	0	0	+	+	+					
Spatula	0	+	+	+	+					
Tablespoon	+	+	+	+	+	+				
Percent Correct	25	50	75	100	100					

The paraprofessional calculated the percent of correct responses that Jacob made during the probes and entered these data on a graph (Figure 3.9). The graph allows Ms. Smith to visually analyze his performance data to determine whether he is making adequate progress toward meeting the objective. In addition, the probe sheet allows Ms. Smith to track his errors on specific words across probe sessions. This information can be used to change the instructional procedures as necessary to provide Jacob more practice on words that are difficult for him.

The probe form shows that Jacob met criterion on the first teaching set on January 18. Ms. Smith then introduced the second teaching set for instruction and planned to probe Jacob's performance on this teaching set on the same schedule. We recommended that previously introduced teaching examples continue to be probed, to ensure that the student is maintaining performance.

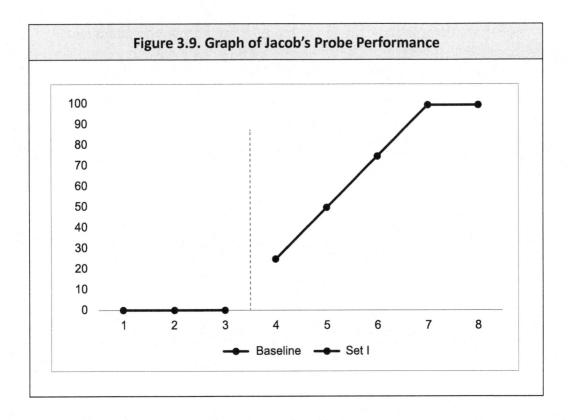

Summary

The components of a teaching plan for EI are similar to those used in most traditional special education instruction approaches. As with all teaching plans, the teacher should employ evidence-based practices tailored to the individual needs of the student and the skill being taught. The difference between EI and traditional instructional programs is that the trials are distributed during classroom activities and routines. Consequently, the teacher must identify natural and supplemental opportunities to provide instruction to the student. In addition, the teacher must ensure that any individual carrying out instruction can reliably identify and take advantage of these opportunities. The teacher must also monitor the student's performance in EI programs. It is recommended that regular probes of student performance be used to accomplish this goal. The frequency of probe sessions should be based on the student's learning history; again, it is better at first to schedule them too often rather than too infrequently, to prevent students from becoming bored if they are mastering the skills quickly or, on the other hand, to prevent them from practicing errors.

CHAPTER 4

Implementing the Embedded Instruction Program

The success of embedded instruction (EI) hinges upon consistent implementation of the teaching plan. The same instructional procedures—presentation sequence, assistance strategy, and reinforcement or error correction—should be implemented with both natural and supplemental embedded instruction trials. In order to achieve this outcome, the teacher must (a) train the instructors (e.g., special education paraprofessionals, student peers) to reliably implement EI, (b) monitor the fidelity of program implementation by instructors, and (c) monitor the number of natural and supplemental embedded instruction trials being presented to the student within and across instructional sessions.

Train Instructors

One of the challenges in successfully implementing EI is ensuring that the individuals carrying it out are taking advantage of all possible opportunities to present instructional trials to the student and are implementing teaching procedures consistently. There are numerous research studies focused on validating procedures for effectively training individuals to implement EI (Jameson, McDonnell, Johnson, Riesen, & Polychronis, 2007; Johnson & McDonnell, 2004; McBride & Schwartz, 2003; VanDerheyden, Snyder, Smith, Sevin, & Longwell, 2005; Wolery et al., 1997). These studies have identified several procedures that can improve the quality and effectiveness of training provided to instructors. These include the teacher providing (a) written materials that describe the procedures to the instructor, (b) modeling and role play prior to implementation of EI in the classroom, and (c) modeling and guided practice in implementing the procedures in the classroom.

Written Materials

Research suggests that instructors benefit from reviewing brief and clearly written materials about EI prior to implementing it with students in the classroom. (See Appendix B for an annotated bibliography of EI research.) In our own work, these materials typically include a description of EI and rationale for its use in the classroom, a description of how EI will be implemented with students, illustrations of when EI trials can be presented to the student, and examples of the teaching plan and data collection forms to be used by the instructor. These materials are used during the training to help communicate what is expected of the instructor and serve as a future reference if the instructor has questions. An example of materials developed to train middle school peers without disabilities to implement EI is provided in Appendix C (Jameson et al., 2007).

Modeling and Role-Play

Another strategy that has proven to be effective is for the teacher to model the procedures during a role-play with the instructor, and then to have the instructor demonstrate the procedures with the teacher acting as student. During this role playing, the teacher should provide the full range of possible responses that a student might make during EI, including correct responses, no responses, or incorrect responses. The teacher should provide ongoing feedback to the instructor on the implementation of the procedures until a prespecified performance criterion (e.g., five consecutive trials without procedural errors) is met.

Modeling and Guided Practice in the Classroom

The final strategy is to model the implementation of EI and provide guided practice to the instructor with the student in the classroom. The teacher first demonstrates the implementation of the strategies laid out in the teaching plan. Next, the instructor implements the strategies with ongoing assistance and feedback from the teacher. Finally, the instructor is asked to implement the strategies without assistance from the teacher. Modeling and guided practice continues until the instructor is able to meet a prespecified performance criterion. A reasonable criterion is 100% accuracy in implementing the teaching plan across two consecutive EI sessions.

Monitor Program Fidelity

A critical implementation issue is whether the EI teaching plan is being implemented consistently and correctly by those providing support to the student. This is important because it is impossible to assess the fundamental effectiveness of the EI program if it is not being implemented the same way across class periods, routines, or activities. Consequently, the teacher must regularly observe the individuals who are implementing the EI program in the general education class.

Figure 4.1 is a sample program monitoring form Ms. Smith used to assess the performance of Jacob's peer instructor, Karen. She wanted Karen to vary the stimulus cards on each supplemental trial with Jacob and to use a 3-second time-delay procedure. She noted on the form that Karen was to implement step 2/2 of the teaching plan with Jacob during the observation. This meant that Karen was supposed to present the second word set (*colander, spoon, whisk, qt*) using a 3-second time delay. Karen provided Jacob with four supplemental trials and one natural trial during the class period.

Figure 4.1. Sample Program Monitoring Form					
Student: Jacob EI Program Step: 2/2					
Instructor: Karen Observer: Ms. Smith Date: 1/17					
Trial	1	2	3	4	5
Program Step	S	N	S	S	S
1. Initiates an instructional trial at planned times or when a natural opportunity occurs.	+	+	+	+	+
2. Varies instructional materials.	+	0	+	+	+
3. Obtains student's attention.	+	+	+	+	+
4. Delivers instructional cue.	+	+	+	+	+
5. Delays controlling prompt.	+	0	+	0	+
6. Delivers controlling prompt.	+	+	+	+	+
7. Provides correct level of reinforcement (unprompted or prompted). OR Implements error correction procedure.	+	+	+	+	+
8. Records trial on tracking form.	+	+	+	+	+
Percent Correct (Total Correct Steps/Total Steps x 100)	37/40 x 100 = 92.5%				

The data indicate that Karen forgot to change the flash cards used to present the words to Jacob in one trial, and that she did not delay the controlling prompt for 3 seconds in two of the trials. Her overall level of fidelity during the class period was 92.5% (37/40 x 100). Although this is a very good level of fidelity, Ms. Smith will need to address the fact that she did not delay the controlling prompt the appropriate amount of time during two of the trials. At this point, she should provide Karen with feedback about the errors and remind her to be sure to delay the controlling prompt. However, if Karen makes the same mistake during her next observation, Ms. Smith may need to provide additional training on implementing the EI program.

To ensure fidelity of program implementation, teachers should try to observe as many trials as possible during a session. The frequency of fidelity observations should be adjusted based on the complexity of the skill being taught and whether the student has unique needs that may influence the efficacy of instruction (e.g., behavior problems, side effects of medications). When an instructor is first learning to implement EI, the teacher should observe more frequently. As the instructor becomes more proficient, the frequency of observation can be reduced to a level that accommodates the student, the skill, and the class.

Track Presentation of Naturalist and Supplemental Trials

In Appendix A, we include a form that is designed to help track the number of natural and supplemental embedded instruction trials provided to a student by an instructor. It serves a dual purpose, as a reminder to the instructor to make sure to provide the number of scheduled trials during each session. In setting up the form, the teacher enters the class periods and activities in which embedded instruction should be implemented with the student, the date of instruction, and the step and phase numbers from the teaching plan. The instructor completes the form, indicating each instance of presenting a natural (N) or supplemental (S) embedded instruction trial to the student during each class, activity, or routine. (This information is usually recorded after each trial is presented to the student.)

For example, as illustrated in Figure 4.2, on January 12, Karen presented the second word set (Step 2) to Jacob and used the zero-second time delay procedure (Phase 1). During the class period, she was able to present a total of six instructional trials, two natural trials, and four supplemental trials.

To make recording easier, the form can be left at the target student's desk and be completed by the instructor during each session. Some instructors find it helpful to carry a small piece of paper or attach a small paper band to their wrist as a reminder to record the number of trials provided to the student. There are also an increasing number of mobile applications available to easily collect and share data using mobile devices (e.g., AccuPoint Big Data, Autism Tracker, Skill Tracker Pro). Following the session, this information can be transferred to forms to allow ongoing tracking by the teacher of the number and type of trials provided to the student within and across sessions.

It is typically not necessary to track the number of trials presented to the student each day. Once or twice a week should be sufficient in most cases to ensure that the student is receiving an adequate number of trials. However, the frequency of data collection should be increased if the data suggest that the number of trials presented to the student is declining. The information gathered on the tracking sheet should be reviewed by the teacher at least weekly to ensure that the student is receiving an adequate number of instructional trials to promote efficient learning.

Figure 4.2. Sample Tracking Sheet

Student: Jacob **Instructor: Karen**

Date/Instructional condition			Class/Activity/Routine									
Date	Step	Phase	Foods Class									
			N	S	N	S	N	S	N	S	N	S
1/11	2	1	✓✓	✓✓ ✓✓								
1/14	2	2	✓	✓✓ ✓✓ ✓✓								
1/15	2	2	✓✓ ✓	✓✓ ✓								
1/16	2	2	✓✓ ✓	✓✓ ✓✓								
1/17	2	2	✓	✓✓ ✓✓								

Summary

The quality of EI can be improved by providing the individual who will be carrying out EI with (a) training on the implementation of the teaching plan, (b) monitoring the fidelity of implementation of the teaching plan, and (c) ensuring that the instructor provides a sufficient number of learning trials each day. Training should focus on the explicit requirements of successfully implementing the EI teaching plan. The teacher should regularly monitor the accuracy of the instructor's implementation of the plan and the frequency of presentation of instructional trials. Instructors who deviate from the teaching plan or the instructional trial schedule need to receive additional training until the fidelity of their implementation improves.

CHAPTER 5

Supporting Student Learning

After implementing an embedded instruction (EI) program, teachers may find it necessary to modify or adjust instructional procedures to ensure that students continue to learn at the expected rate. Decisions about how to change the instructional procedures should be determined by the patterns in graphed student performance data. Research has consistently shown that students achieve greater instructional success with teachers who use data to adjust instructional procedures than with teachers who do not (Collins, 2012; Haring, Liberty, & White, 1980; Snell & Lloyd, 1991).

Problem Data Patterns

There are four patterns in graphed data that should raise red flags for teachers as they carry out their regular reviews of student performance in EI programs. These are (a) slow improvements in performance, (b) variable performance, (c) flat performance, and (d) decreasing performance. Teachers can use these patterns to help narrow the range of possible explanations for why a student is not making progress as expected in the instructional program.

Slow Improvements in Performance

In this pattern (Figure 5.1), the student's performance is improving at a rate slower than expected. There are many factors that might affect how quickly a student learns a new skill., When this problem arises in EI programs, however, it often means that the instructional task is too difficult for the student. This may occur when the teacher is presenting too many instructional examples at one time, or when the student lacks adequate prerequisite skills to complete the response. For example, if Ms. Smith saw this pattern with Jacob, it could mean that she had included too many words and symbols in the teaching sets, or that he did not have the necessary discrimination skills to differentiate between the words and symbols. In Lisa's case, this problem could arise because too many symbols had been placed on her speech-generating device, resulting in difficulty discriminating among them. Alternatively, the symbols might not have been located in the right position on the device to allow her to successfully access or depress the button.

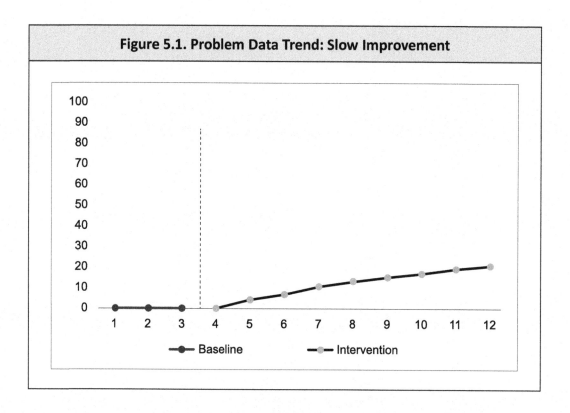

Figure 5.1. Problem Data Trend: Slow Improvement

Variable Performance Across Probe Sessions

This data pattern (Figure 5.2) can result when the conditions under which the student is learning the new skill are changing from one instructional session to the next while the instructional procedures have not been designed to accommodate this variation. This variation could occur within a class period or across class periods.

For example, Jacob's performance might vary if most of the instructional trials he receives are provided during independent seat work times versus during lab activities. His performance might be better during independent seat work activities because there are fewer distractions than during lab activities. Variability in the data may also result from instructor variability, either in implementing program procedures or in applying definitions of correct and incorrect responses.

Chapter 5

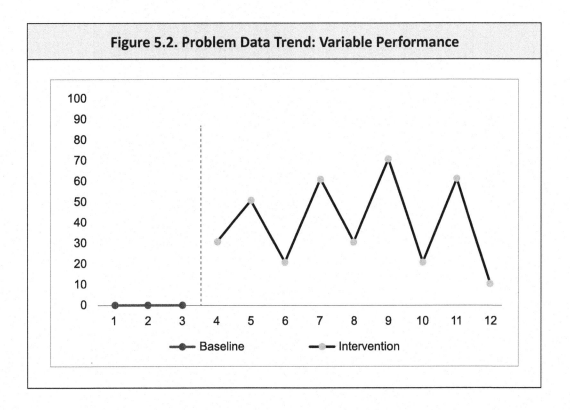

Figure 5.2. Problem Data Trend: Variable Performance

Flat Performance Across Probe Sessions

In this situation, the student's performance initially improves but then stagnates and remains at the same level across multiple probe sessions (see Figure 5.3). There are two likely explanations for this type of pattern. First, the student is consistently making errors on one or more of the examples included in the teaching plan; the student's overall performance does not improve because she is making mistakes on the same example over and over again. Second, the student may have learned to wait for the teacher's assistance rather than trying to respond independently. For example, if Jacob learned to read *tongs* and *spatula* in the first teaching set, the data would indicate that his performance improved from 0% to 50% correct. If he continued to miss the other two words included in the teaching set, the data pattern would remain flat at 50% across probe sessions. Ms. Smith would see a similar data pattern if Jacob had learned to wait for her assistance on these words rather than trying to read them by himself.

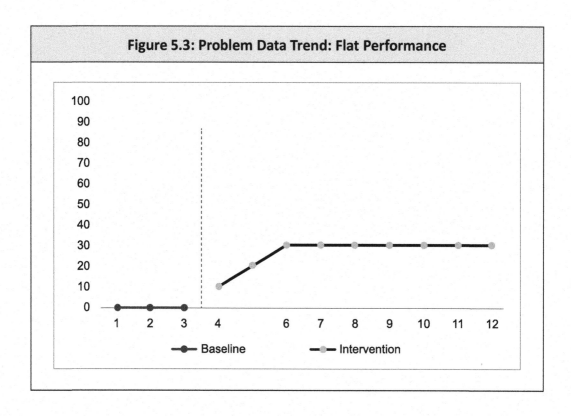

Decreasing Performance Across Probe Sessions

When the student's performance initially improves and then declines after several probe sessions (Figure 5.4), it often suggests that the student is bored. The instructional procedures will need to be modified to make the instructional task more interesting or more reinforcing for the student to stay engaged in the task. This data pattern can also emerge if the student is not receiving enough instructional trials to maintain performance on previously learned examples.

Modifying Instructional Procedures

Modifications or adjustments to the instructional procedures can focus on four key components of the EI program. These include (a) the amount of practice the student is provided, (b) the composition and structure of the teaching set or response, (c) the assistance that the teacher provides to the student, and (d) the strategies used to reinforce the student's unprompted correct responses.

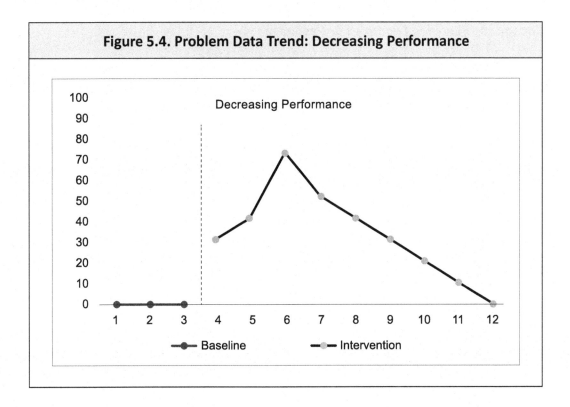

Figure 5.4. Problem Data Trend: Decreasing Performance

Change the Amount of Practice

There are three possible modifications or adjustments teachers can make to ensure that students are getting the amount of practice they need to learn a skill. First, the teacher can increase the total number of instructional trials that the student receives during each class period or activity. The teacher may have initially underestimated the number of trials that the student would need to learn a new skill. Second, the teacher may need to focus the majority of instructional trials provided to the student on more difficult examples. As instruction proceeds, it is common to see students learn some of the examples included in the set more quickly than others. When this occurs, the teacher might note the kinds of examples on which the student makes errors, and then focus subsequent instructional trials on similar examples.

Finally, the teacher may need to modify teaching procedures to ensure that the student receives a consistent number of instructional trials each day. A student's learning may be hampered when there are, say, 10 presentations of the teaching set on Monday, three presentations on Tuesday, one presentation on Wednesday, and so on.

Change the Teaching Examples or Response

Student performance data may suggest that the teacher should modify the teaching set or alter the specific response that the student is required to make during instructional trials. Experience suggests that there are four possible changes that the teacher might make to improve student learning. First, the teacher may reduce or increase the total number of examples included in the teaching set. Teachers typically reduce the number of examples included in the teaching set when a student's rate of learning does not match expectations. The objective is to reduce the difficulty of the instructional task for the student and to increase the overall level of success during instructional sessions. Conversely, the teacher may increase the number of examples in the teaching set if it is too easy for the student or if the student is becoming bored with the instructional task. The goal is to make sure that the instructional task stays interesting and challenging to the student.

Second, the teacher might reorganize the teaching sets so that difficult examples are spread out over instructional sessions. For example, if the student is making a large number of errors on three examples included in a teaching set, the teacher might reorganize the set so that the two most difficult examples are taken out of the set, and then reintroduced one at a time as the student's performance improves.

Third, the teacher can change the instructional materials to help the student learn difficult examples. For example, in Jacob's Foods class Ms. Smith might initially pair a written word (e.g., *spatula*) or symbol with pictures of the object. After Jacob is consistently reading the word or symbol name when presented with the picture, Ms. Smith might delay the presentation of the picture to give him an opportunity to read the word independently.

Finally, the teacher can simplify or modify the expected response so that it matches the student's ability. This might mean changing the type of response that the student makes during instructional trials. For example, in the foods class a student could point to the object when shown the written word or symbol rather than reading it aloud. The teacher could also develop an alternative response that achieves the same outcome for the student. Thus, in the foods class, the teacher could require the student to complete recipes using photographs of the required steps rather than reading a written recipe.

Change Assistance Strategies

Teachers also can alter the response prompting and fading procedures being used to provide assistance to the student. For example, if Jacob consistently made a large number of errors when Ms. Smith moved from the zero-second delay to the 3-second delay, she might shorten the delay interval or change to a progressive time-delay procedure allowing the delay interval to be gradually increased across trials or sessions. Similarly, if the data suggested that Lisa was inadvertently being taught to wait for prompts to activate her communication device, Mrs. Wright might switch to a constant time-delay procedure and reinforce her self-initiated responses.

Change the Reinforcement Strategy

The final component of the teaching plan that often must be adjusted is the reinforcement procedures. These changes can ensure that the student receives salient performance feedback by heightening the contrast between consequences for different types of response—unprompted correct, prompted correct, and incorrect—and can thus maintain student motivation during instruction. It is common for teachers to systematically change the amount, the frequency, or the type of reinforcement provided. In most cases, the teacher will reinforce the student following each unprompted correct response during the initial stages of the instruction. Perhaps the most frequent change is to increase the amount of reinforcement the student receives following a correct response.

Another option is to develop a menu of reinforcers that is available to the student for correct responding during instructional sessions. This change is often needed if the student is losing interest in the instructional task or the particular reinforcer. The teacher might identify a variety of activity reinforcers specific to the student's preferences (e.g., listening to music, reading a book, feeding the class pet), any of which are available if the student is engaged in the instructional task and achieves a certain level of performance during the session.

Troubleshooting

Teachers should use a five-step process to troubleshoot EI programs. These steps are as follows.

Step 1: Identify the Data Pattern

Once the teacher is sure that the student's performance is not due to other contextual factors, the teacher should identify whether the student's performance data indicates (a) slow improvements in performance, (b) variable performance, (c) flat performance, or (d) decreasing performance. We recommend that this decision be based on data from 10 consecutive probe sessions unless responses are consistently incorrect. This amount of data is often necessary to establish a clear pattern in the student's performance.

Step 2: Eliminate Other Contextual Explanations

Once the teacher is confident that the teaching plan is being implemented correctly, the next step is to make sure that other contextual problems are not negatively impacting the student's performance. For example, the number of instructional trials presented to a student could be affected by changes in the routines or activities of the general education class. Other factors, such as student health problems, can also affect how quickly a student learns a skill. The teacher should eliminate these factors as potential reasons for a student's performance before altering the EI program.

Step 3: Assess the Consistency of Program Implementation

The teacher should ensure that the staff is consistently implementing the teaching plan before making significant efforts to change the procedures. Poor student performance may result when the person carrying out the plan does not consistently present the controlling prompt across instructional trials or sessions. Similarly, the rate of learning may be affected if different staff members use different procedures to teach the same skill to a student.

The way to avoid this problem is for teachers to regularly observe and provide feedback to staff about their implementation of the EI program. Teachers should ensure that the program is being implemented correctly for at least two consecutive observations before considering any changes in the teaching plan.

Step 4: Identify a Potential Hypothesis

After identifying a consistent pattern in student performance, teachers can use our EI troubleshooting matrix (Table 5.1) to develop one or more hypotheses about why a student is not making adequate progress. The matrix provides a general guide for teachers to determine which components of the teaching plan should be changed. The teacher can develop a hypothesis by reviewing their EI probe, data collection, and tracking sheets, and observing the student during instruction. An examination of the tracking sheet (see Chapter 4) allows the teacher to assess whether the student is receiving a consistent number of instructional trials each day and whether the amount of practice opportunities needs to be increased.

Teachers should also examine the raw data from their probe sheets to identify whether students are having problems with specific examples included in the teaching plan and, if possible, to identify the type of error(s) that students are making. Identifying specific error patterns in the raw data can in turn help teachers identify ways to modify the instructional materials presented to students or the type of assistance provided during instruction.

Table 5.1. Troubleshooting Matrix

Data pattern and potential problem	Possible modifications			
	Amount of practice	Teaching examples or response	Assistance strategies	Reinforcement strategies
Slow improvement in performance *Potential problem*: The instructional task is too difficult for the student.	Increase the number of instructional trials.	• Reduce the number of examples in a set. • Simplify the response or develop an alternative response.	Change the controlling prompt to provide more assistance.	• Increase the amount of reinforcement for unprompted responses. • Increase the frequency of reinforcement for unprompted response.
Variable performance *Potential problem*: The instructional procedures are not compatible with all variations in the ongoing classroom routines or activities.	Ensure that a consistent number of trials is presented across sessions.	Change the teaching examples or response to ensure compatibility with ongoing routines and activities.	Change the instructional cues or controlling prompt to ensure compatibility with ongoing routines and activities.	• Increase the amount of reinforcement for unprompted responses. • Increase the frequency of reinforcement for unprompted responses.
Flat performance *Potential problems*: • The student is making consistent errors on specific examples. • The student is becoming dependent upon the controlling prompt.	Provide additional instruction trials on difficult examples.	• Reduce the number of difficult examples in the set. • Change the instructional materials to highlight the critical features of difficult examples.	• Modify the assistance procedure to provide more assistance to the student and reduce error rates. • Change the fading procedure to reflect student performance and the skill.	• Increase the amount of reinforcement for unprompted responses. • Increase the frequency of reinforcement for unprompted responses.
Decreasing performance *Potential problem*: The student is bored because the instructional task is too easy.	Increase the number of instructional trials.	• Increase the number of examples included in the teaching set. • Increase the difficulty of the examples included in the teaching set.	Change the controlling prompt to provide less assistance.	• Develop a menu of reinforcers and vary them across sessions. • Increase the amount of reinforcement for unprompted responses. • Increase the frequency of reinforcement for unprompted responses.

Finally, teachers should observe students' behavior. This allows teachers to assess the effectiveness of the assistance and reinforcement strategies.

Any hypotheses regarding student performance should be shared with the general education teacher and with other individuals implementing the EI program. This process helps to obtain a consensus on (a) what is causing the student's problems and (b) any specific changes that should be made to the teaching plan.

Step 5: Change the Teaching Plan

When making modifications or adaptations, teachers should complete a new teaching plan form, review the changes with any individuals implementing the program, and provide additional training as necessary to ensure correct and consistent implementation of the new procedures. Finally, teachers should note when the changes in teaching plan are put into place on graphs of the students' probe performance.

Summary

No teaching plan is perfect. Teachers should continuously review and adjust the teaching procedures in response to the student performance and to changes in the general education class. The focus should be on ensuring that students are making continuous progress in acquiring a skill. This can be accomplished by using student performance data to identify potential problems, developing a hypothesis about why the problem is occurring, and then adjusting one or more components of the teaching plan. As with all aspects of EI, adjustments to the teaching plan should be done collaboratively with the student's individualized education program team members.

References

Barbetta, P. M., Heron, T. E., & Heward, W. L. (1993). Effects of active student response during error correction on the acquisition, maintenance, and generalization of sight words by students with developmental disabilities. *Journal of Applied Behavior Analysis, 26*, 111–119. doi:10.1901/jaba.1993.26-111

Barbetta, P. M., Heward, W. L., Bradley, D. M., & Miller, A. D. (1994). Effects of immediate and delayed error correction on the acquisition and maintenance of sight words by students with developmental disabilities. *Journal of Applied Behavior Analysis, 27*, 177–178. doi:10.1901/jaba.1994.27-177

Brophy, J. E., & Good, T. L. (1986). Teacher behavior and student achievement. In M. C. Wittrock (Ed.), *Handbook of research on teaching* (3rd ed., pp. 328–375). New York, NY: MacMillan.

Clark, L.S., Haydon, T., Bauer, A., & Epperly, A.C. (2016). Inclusion of students with an intellectual disability in the general education classroom with the use of response cards. *Preventing School Failure: Alternative Education for Children and Youth, 60,* 1, 35-42. doi: 10.1080/1045988x.2014.966801

Collins, B. C. (2012). *Systematic instruction for students with moderate and severe disabilities*. Baltimore, MD: Paul H. Brookes.

Farlow, L. J., & Snell, M. E. (1994). *Making the most of student performance data*. Washington, D.C.: American Association on Mental Retardation.

Giangreco, M. F., Dennis, R., Cloninger, C. J., Edelman, S., & Schattman, R. (1993). "I've counted Jon": Transformational experiences of teachers educating students with disabilities. *Exceptional Children, 59*, 359–372. doi:10.1177/001440299305900408

Greenwood, C. R., Delquadri, J., & Hall, R. V. (1984). Opportunity to respond and student academic performance. In W. L. Heward, T. E. Heron, J. Trapp-Porter, & D. S. Hill (Eds.), *Focus on behavior analysis in education* (pp. 58–88). Columbus, OH: Charles Merrill.

Haring, N., Liberty, K., & White, O. R. (1980). Rules for data-based strategy decisions in instructional programs: Current research and implications. In W. Sailor, B. Wilcox, & L. Brown (Eds.), *Methods of instruction for severely handicapped learners* (pp. 159–162). Baltimore, MD: Paul H. Brookes.

Horner, R. H., McDonnell, J. J., & Bellamy, G. T. (1986). Teaching generalized skills: General case instruction in simulation and community settings. In R. H. Horner, L. H. Meyer, and H. D. Fredericks (Eds.), *Education of learners with severe handicaps: Exemplary service strategies* (pp. 289–214). Baltimore, MD: Paul H. Brookes.

Horner, R. H., Williams, J. A., & Knobbe, C. (1985). The effect of "opportunity to perform" on the maintenance of skills learned by high school students with severe handicaps. *Journal of the Association for Persons with Severe Handicaps, 10*, 172–175. doi:10.1177/154079698501000308

Hunt, P., Doering, K., Hirose-Hatae, A., Maier, J., & Goetz, L. (2001). Across-person collaboration to support students with and without disabilities in a general education classroom. *Journal of the Association for Persons with Severe Handicaps, 26*, 240–256. doi:10.2511/rpsd.26.4.240

Hunt, P., & McDonnell, J. (2007). Inclusive education. In S. L. Odom, R. H. Horner, M. Snell, and J. Blacher (Eds.), *Handbook on Developmental Disabilities* (pp. 269–291). New York, NY: Guilford.

Hunt, P., McDonnell, J., & Crockett, M. A. (2012). Reconciling an ecological curricular framework focusing on quality of life outcomes with the development and instruction of standards-based academic goals. *Research and Practice for Persons with Severe Disabilities, 37*, 3, 139–152. doi:10.2511/027494812804153471

Hunt, P., Soto, G., Maier, J., & Doering, K. (2003). Collaborative teaming to support students at risk and students with severe disabilities in general education classrooms. *Exceptional Children, 69*, 315–332. doi:10.1177/001440290306900304

Jameson, J. M., McDonnell, J., Johnson, J. W., Riesen, T., & Polychronis, S. (2007). A comparison of one-to-one embedded instruction in the general education classroom and one-to-one massed practice instruction the special education classroom. *Education and Treatment of Children, 30*, 23–44. doi:10.1353/etc.2007.0001

Jimenez, B. A., & Kamei, A. (2015). Embedded instruction: An evaluation of evidence to inform inclusive practice. *Inclusion*, 132–144. doi:10.1352/2326-6988-3.3.132

Johnson, J. W., & McDonnell, J. (2004). An exploratory study of the implementation of embedded instruction by general educators with students with developmental disabilities. *Education and Treatment of Children, 27*, 46–63.

References

Johnson, J. W., McDonnell, J., Holzwarth, V., & Hunter, K. (2004). The efficacy of embedded instruction for students with developmental disabilities enrolled in general education classes. *Journal of Positive Behavioral Interventions, 6*, 214–227. doi:10.1177/10983007040060040301

McBride, B. J., & Schwartz, I. S. (2003). Effects of teaching early interventionists to use discrete trials during ongoing classroom activities. *Topics in Early Childhood Special Education, 23*, 5–17. doi:10.1177/027112140302300102

McDonnell, J., & Hunt, P. (2014). Inclusive education and meaningful school outcomes (pp. 155–176). In M. Agran, F. Brown, C. Hughes, C. Quirk, & D. Ryndak (Eds.), *Equity and full participation for individuals with severe disabilities*. Baltimore, MD: Paul H. Brooks.

McDonnell, J., Jameson, J.M., Bowman, J., Coleman, O., Ryan, J., Eichelberger, C., and Conradi, L. (In press). Assessing generalization is single-case research studies teaching core academic content to students with intellectual and developmental disabilities. *Focus on Autism and Other Intellectual Disabilities.*

McDonnell, J., Jameson, M. J., Riesen, T., & Polychronis, P. (2014). Embedded instruction in inclusive settings. In D. M. Browder & F. Spooner (Eds.), *Language arts, math, and science for students with significant cognitive disabilities* (pp. 15–36). Baltimore, MD: Paul H. Brookes.

McDonnell, J., Johnson, J. W., Polychronis, S., & Riesen, T. (2002). The effects of embedded instruction on students with moderate disabilities enrolled in general education classes. *Education and Training in Mental Retardation and Developmental Disabilities, 37*, 363–377.

McDonnell, J., Snell, M., Brown, F., Coleman, O., & Eichelberger, C. (2019). Individualized instructional strategies. In F. Brown, J. McDonnell, & M. Snell (Eds.), *Instruction of students with severe disabilities* (9th ed., pp. 156-206). New York, NY: Pearson.

McDonnell, J. J., & Ferguson, B. (1988). A comparison of general case in vivo and general case simulation plus in vivo training. *Journal of the Association for Persons with Severe Handicaps, 13*, 116–124. doi:10.1177/154079698801300208

Morningstar, M., Kurth, J., & Johnson P.E. (2017). Examining national trends in educational placement for students with significant disabilities. *Remedial and Special Education, 38*, 3–12. doi:10.1177/0741932516678327

Reynolds, A. J. (1991). Early schooling of children at risk. *American Educational Research Journal, 28*, 392–442. doi:10.3102/00028312028002392

Riesen, T., McDonnell, J., Johnson, J. W., Polychronis, S., & Jameson, M. (2003). A comparison of time delay and simultaneous prompting within embedded instruction in general education classes with students with moderate to severe disabilities. *Journal of Behavioral Education, 12*, 241–260. doi:10.1023/A:1026076406656

Rosenshine, B., & Stevens, R. (1986). Teaching functions. In M. C. Wittrock (Ed.), *Handbook on research on teaching* (3rd ed., pp. 376–391). New York: Macmillian.

Rosenthal-Malek, A., & Bloom, A. (1998). Beyond acquisition: Teaching generalization for students with developmental disabilities. In A. Hilton & R. Ringlaben (Eds.), *Best and promising practices in developmental disabilities* (pp. 139–155). Austin, TX: PRO-ED.

Ryndak, D., Orlando, A. M., & Burnett, K. (2019). Designing and implementing instruction for inclusive classes. In F. E. Brown, J. McDonnell, & M. Snell (Eds.), *Instruction of students with severe disabilities* (9th ed., pp. 207-231). New York, NY: Pearson.

Salisbury, C. L., Evans, I. M., & Palombaro, M. M. (1997). Collaborative problem-solving to promote the inclusion of young children with significant disabilities in primary grades. *Exceptional Children, 63*, 195–209. doi:10.1177/001440299706300204

Schuster, J. W., Hemmeter, M. L., & Ault, M. J. (2001). Instruction of students with moderate and severe disabilities in elementary classrooms. *Early Childhood Research Quarterly, 16*, 329–341. doi:10.1016/S0885-2006(01)00112-0

Singer-Dudek, J., & Greer, R.D. (2005). A long-term analysis of the relationship between fluency and the training and maintenance of complex math skills. *The Psychological Record, 55*, 361–376. doi:10.1007/BF03395516

Snell, M. E., & Lloyd, B. H. (1991). A study of the effects of trend, variability, frequency, and form of data on teachers' judgments about progress and their decisions about program change. *Research in Developmental Disabilities, 12*, 41–62. doi:10.1016/0891-4222(91)90022-K

VanDerHeyden, A. M., Snyder, P., Smith, A., Sevin, B., & Longwell, J. (2005). Effects of complete learning trails on child engagement. *Topics in Early Childhood Special Education, 25*, 81–94. doi:10.1177/02711214050250020501

Westling, D. L., & Fox, L. (2004). *Teaching students with severe disabilities* (3rd ed.). Upper Saddle River, NJ: Merrill.

Wolery, M., Anthony, L., Snyder, E. D., Werts, M., & Katzenmeyer, J. (1997). Training elementary teachers to embed instruction during classroom activities. *Education and Treatment of Children, 20*(1), 40–58.

References

Wolery, M., Ault, M. J., & Doyle, P. M. (1992). *Teaching students with moderate to severe disabilities: Use of response prompting strategies*. New York, NY: Longman.

Wolery, M., Bailey, D. B., & Sugai, G. M. (1988). *Effective teaching: Principles and procedures of applied behavior analysis with exceptional students*. Boston, MA: Allyn & Bacon.

York-Barr, J., Schultz, T., Doyle, M. B., Kronberg, R., & Crossett, S. (1996). Inclusive schooling in St. Cloud. *Remedial and Special Education, 17*, 92–105. doi:10.1177/074193259601700205

Appendices

Appendix A: Forms

Baseline Probe Form							
Student:			**Teacher:**				
Instructional cue:							
Example							
	+/0	Prompt	+/0	Prompt	+/0	Prompt

Trial Distribution Planning Form

Student: **Teacher:**

Potential teaching opportunities		Class/Activity/Routine					Total opportunities
Supplemental instructional trials	Activity transitions (opening to lecture; lecture to individual or group activities; going to lab)						
	Natural breaks in activities (lab)						
	Management tasks (roll; distribution of graded assignments)						
	Independent work						
Natural instructional trials							
	Potential opportunities						

Embedded Instruction Teaching Plan

Student:

Instructional objective:

Supplemental instruction opportunities	Natural instruction opportunities

Presentation sequence:

Assistance strategy:

Reinforcement procedures:

Error-correction procedures:

Probe Sheet

Student:				Teacher:						
Example/Item	DATE									
Percent Correct										

Prompt Key: V – Verbal   M – Model   G – Gesture/Point   P – Prime   F – Full Physical

Appendices

Program Monitoring Form						
Student: EI Program Step:						
Instructor: Observer: Date:						
Program Step	Trial					
Percent Correct (Total Correct Steps/Total Steps x 100)						

Instructions: The first column includes the steps of the teaching plan designed for the student. The specific steps included in this column can be adjusted to reflect variations in response prompting and fading procedures, error correction procedures, and so on. The **program step** rows indicate both the trial number and whether the trial was a natural (N) or supplemental (S) embedded instructional trial. Enter "+" or "0" in the box for each trial to reflect whether the instructor's teaching behavior was consistent with the procedures laid out in the teaching plan. Following the observation, calculate the instructor's overall level of fidelity by calculating the percentage of program steps implemented correctly.

Embedded Instruction Tracking Sheet

Student: **Instructor:**

Date/Instructional condition			Class/Activity/Routine									
Date	Step	Phase										
			N	S	N	S	N	S	N	S	N	S

Instructions: Under Class/Activity/Routine, enter the class periods and activities in which embedded instruction should be implemented with the student. You can list up to five activities or routines in which EI is carried out during the day. The step number and phase number are from the teaching plan. The instructor should enter a check mark or tally mark in the box each time they present a natural (N) or supplemental (S) trial to the student.

Appendix B: Annotated Bibliography of Embedded Instruction Research

Embedded instruction commonly refers to explicit, teacher controlled systematic instruction designed to distribute instructional trials within the ongoing routines and activities of inclusive general education settings. The specific instructional procedures used during EI vary based on (a) the needs of the individual student, (b) the skill being taught, and (c) the context in which instruction is being provided. The seminal research studies on EI include:

McDonnell, J. (1998). Instruction for students with severe disabilities in general education settings. *Education and Training in Mental Retardation and Developmental Disabilities, 33*, 199–215.

McDonnell, J., Johnson, J. W., Polychronis, S., & Riesen, T. (2002). The effects of embedded instruction on students with moderate disabilities enrolled in general education classes. *Education and Training in Mental Retardation and Developmental Disabilities, 37*, 363–377.

Rule, S., Losardo, A., Dinnebeil, L., Kaiser, A., & Rowland, C. (1998). Translating research on naturalistic instruction into practice. *Journal of Early Intervention, 21*, 283–293. doi:10.1177/105381519802100401

Schepis, M. M., Reid, D. H., Ownbey, J., & Parsons, M. B. (2001). Training support staff to embed teaching within natural routines of young children with disabilities in an inclusive preschool. *Journal of Applied Behavior Analysis, 34*, 313–327. doi:10.1901/jaba.2001.34-313

Wolery, M., Ault, M. J., & Doyle, P. M. (1992). *Teaching students with moderate to severe disabilities: Use of response prompting strategies.* New York, NY: Longman.

Evidence Base for Embedded Instruction for Students with Developmental and Intellectual Disabilities in General Education Elementary and Middle School Settings: Selected Studies

Wolery, M., Anthony, L., Snyder, E. D., Werts, M., & Katzenmeyer, J. (1997). Training elementary teachers to embed instruction during classroom activities. *Education and Treatment of Children, 20*, 40–58.

Researchers taught general education teachers to use EI with three students with severe disabilities who were included in general education elementary classes. The teachers used a constant time delay procedure to embed instruction for students within the lessons being provided to students without disabilities in the class. The skills that were taught included reading sight words during language arts instruction, naming the days of the week on which selected activities occurred during classroom activities, and categorizing specific foods within the appropriate food group during science class. Results showed that students learned the targeted skills, and general educators were able to successfully implement EI within the activities and routines in the general education class.

Johnson, J. W., McDonnell, J., Holzwarth, V., & Hunter, K. (2004). The efficacy of embedded instruction for students with developmental disabilities enrolled in general education classes. *Journal of Positive Behavioral Interventions, 6*, 214–227. doi:10.1177/10983007040060040301

> Researchers used a multiple baseline across behaviors design to evaluate the efficacy of embedded instruction with three students with intellectual and developmental disabilities who were enrolled in general education classes. Two general education teachers and one paraprofessional delivered embedded instruction to students during regularly scheduled instructional activities. The skills taught to students included answering probe questions drawn from the regular science curriculum, identifying functional sight-words drawn from the regular reading curriculum, and making requests using an electronic communication device. The data showed that embedded instruction was effective with all three students. The results also indicate that both general education teachers and the paraprofessional were able to implement the procedure with a high degree of fidelity without disrupting the ongoing instructional activities of the general education classes. Teacher ratings of the acceptability and perceived effectiveness of the procedures suggested that they viewed embedded instruction as a practical, effective, and efficient strategy for teaching students with intellectual and developmental disabilities in general education settings.

McDonnell, J., Johnson, J. W., Polychronis, S., & Riesen, T. (2002). The effects of embedded instruction on students with moderate disabilities enrolled in general education classes. *Education and Training in Mental Retardation and Developmental Disabilities, 37*, 363–377.

> Researchers used a multiple baseline across behaviors design to evaluate the efficacy of embedded instruction with four junior high school students with developmental disabilities. The study was designed to examine whether paraprofessional staff could successfully implement EI as part of their responsibilities in supporting the participation of students in the class. In addition, the study focused on teaching skills drawn directly from (a) the general education curriculum, and (b) the lessons being presented to students without disabilities. Students were taught to read or define words that were included on vocabulary lists of several general education classes including a food and nutrition class, a health class, and a computer class. EI was carried out by special education paraprofessional staff assigned to support the students in their classes. The results indicated that EI led to the acquisition

and maintenance of the target skills. The paraprofessionals implemented the embedded instruction procedures in general education classes with high levels of procedural fidelity. The students' general education teachers and the paraprofessionals reported that EI was an effective and acceptable strategy for supporting their participation in the general education curriculum.

Johnson, J. W., & McDonnell, J. (2004). An exploratory study of the implementation of embedded instruction by general educators with students with developmental disabilities. *Education and Treatment of Children, 27*, 46–63.

This exploratory study suggested that EI is an effective strategy for teaching skills to elementary and middle school age students that are drawn either from their IEP or from the general education curriculum. The general educators, paraprofessionals, and peers without disabilities who participated in the studies learned to implement EI with a limited amount of training and ongoing support. These studies also concluded that while EI consistently produced student learning, it is also perceived by teachers, paraprofessionals, and peers as being an acceptable approach compatible with the typical instructional activities of general education classes.

Hudson, M. E., Browder, D. M., & Wood, L. A. (2013). Review of experimental research on academic learning by students with moderate and severe intellectual disability in general education. *Research and Practice for Persons with Severe Disabilities, 38*, 1, 17–29. doi:10.2511/027494813807046926

Researchers reviewed the literature on academic learning in general education settings for students with moderate and severe intellectual disability was conducted. A total of 17 experimental studies was identified and evaluated using quality indicators for single-case design research. Studies that met or met with reservation the criteria established for quality research were used to determine the evidence base of the instructional strategies described in the literature. The review found embedded instruction trials using constant time delay to be an evidence-based practice for teaching academic content to students with moderate and severe intellectual disability in general education.

McDonnell, J., Johnson, J. W., Polychronis, S., Riesen, T., Jameson, J. M., & Kercher, K. (2006). A comparison of one-to-one embedded instruction in general education classes with small group instruction in special education classes. *Education and Training in Developmental Disabilities, 41*, 125–138.

Jameson, J. M., McDonnell, J., Johnson, J. W., Riesen, T., & Polychronis, S. (2007). A comparison of one-to-one embedded instruction in the general education classroom and one-to-one massed practice instruction the special education classroom. *Education and Treatment of Children, 30*, 23-44. doi:10.1353/etc.2007.0001

McDonnell and colleagues compared the effectiveness of embedded instruction in general education classes and small-group instruction in special education classes to teach vocabulary word definitions to four middle school students with intellectual and developmental disabilities. In addition, this study examined the extent to which the two instructional formats led to the generalization of students' performance to materials typically used in the general education classes (i.e., teacher developed worksheets, textbooks). The results showed that embedded and small-group instruction were equally effective in promoting the acquisition and generalization of the target skill.

Jameson and colleagues compared the relative effectiveness of one-on-one embedded instruction in general educations classrooms with one-on-one massed-trial instruction in a special education class with four middle school students with intellectual and developmental disabilities. The results indicate that both instructional formats were effective in promoting the acquisition of the target skills. However, the data showed that one-to-one massed-trial instruction was slightly more effective for two of the students, one-to-one embedded instruction was more effective for one student, and the two strategies were equally effective for the last student.

Jameson, M., & McDonnell, J. (2007). *Embedded constant time delay instruction by peers without disabilities in general education classrooms*. Salt Lake City, UT: Department of Special Education, University of Utah.

The purpose of the study was to determine if peers without disabilities enrolled in the same class could successfully implement EI with students with disabilities, and whether they could generalize the implementation of EI to similar instructional activities without assistance or feedback. Students without disabilities were taught to implement EI in a 30-min training session prior to the implementation of the study and were provided on-going feedback about their implementation of EI on one set of concepts throughout the study. The results showed that students with disabilities learned the target skills when receiving instruction from peers without disabilities. The results also demonstrated that peers without disabilities could implement EI with a high degree of procedural fidelity, and successfully generalize the implementation of EI procedures to similar instructional activities without assistance or feedback. Finally, the students without disabilities and their general education teachers reported that EI was an effective and acceptable strategy for providing instruction to students within the on-going routines of the general education classes.

Research on Key Procedural Components of Embedded Instruction: Response Prompting, Trial Distribution, and Higher Order Learning Strategies.

Riesen, T., McDonnell, J., Johnson, J. W., Polychronis, S., & Jameson, M. (2003). A comparison of time delay and simultaneous prompting within embedded instruction in general education classes with students with moderate to severe disabilities. *Journal of Behavioral Education, 12,* 241–260. doi:10.1023/A:1026076406656

> Researchers compared CTD time delay and simultaneous prompting procedures within an embedded instruction format to teach academic skills to four middle school students with disabilities. Paraprofessionals used CTD to teach one set of vocabulary words and simultaneous prompting to teach another set. The number of instructional trials provided to students was controlled under both conditions. The results of the study showed that both procedures were effective in promoting the acquisition of the target skills. However, the constant time delay procedure was more effective for two of the students and the simultaneous prompting procedure was more effective for the remaining two students. The paraprofessionals implemented embedded instruction with a high degree of procedural fidelity regardless of the response prompting and fading procedure used.

Johnson, J. W., McDonnell, J., Holzwarth, V., & Berry, R. (2007). *Using embedded instruction to teach students with developmental disabilities in general education classes: a comparison of simultaneous prompting and the system of most prompts.* Dekalb, IL: Northern Illinois University.

> Researchers compared the effectiveness of CTD and the system of least prompts in teaching basic academic skills to four elementary students with developmental disabilities. Two general education teachers and two paraprofessionals provided EI using CTD and the system of least prompts to the students in their general education classrooms. The results showed that both procedures led to the acquisition of the target skills for all three students. For two students, the system of most prompts was more efficient in terms of rate of acquisition and number of trials to criterion. Simultaneous prompting was slightly more efficient in terms of trials to criterion for the third student. The paraprofessionals were able to implement both procedures with a high degree of fidelity, and rated both procedures as equally effective and efficient.

Polychronis, S. C., McDonnell, J., Johnson, J. W., Riesen, T., & Jameson, M. (2004). A comparison of two trial distribution schedules in embedded instruction. *Focus on Autism and Other Developmental Disabilities, 19,* 140–151. doi:10.1177/10883 576040190030201

> Researchers examined the effectiveness of two trial distribution schedules implemented in an embedded instruction package to teach academic skills to four elementary students with developmental disabilities in general education classes. In the first package, instructional trials were distributed across a 30-min time period that reflected the typical length of a lesson in the content area (e.g., math or reading). In the second package, instructional trials were distributed across a 120-min time period that cut across at least two lessons

(e.g., math and reading). General education teachers provided instruction to students under both trial distribution conditions. The results indicated that both schedules lead to the acquisition of the target skills. In addition, students were able to generalize their performance to natural stimuli found in general education classes. However, the 30-min trial distribution schedule resulted in faster acquisition of the skills for two of the students. There were no substantial differences in the rates of acquisition under the two schedules for the other two students. In analyzing the data more closely, researchers found that the two students with more significant disabilities learned the skills more quickly when the trials were distributed with a 30-min schedule than when they were distributed over a longer time period.

Jameson, J. M., Walker, R., Utley, K., & Maughan, R. (2012). A comparison of embedded total task instruction in teaching behavioral chains to massed one-on-one instruction for students with intellectual disabilities: Accessing general education settings and core academic content. Behavior Modification, 36, 320–340. doi:10.1177/0145445512440574

> Researchers compared the embedded instruction of behavioral chains with more traditional (one-on-one massed trials in special education setting) instructional procedures for teaching behavioral chains to students with significant cognitive disabilities. The chains targeted for instruction were selected by state core educational needs and functional skill development. Results indicated that students learned the behavioral chains using inclusive embedded instruction as quickly, or in less time, than more traditional instructional formats. In addition social validity ratings from general and special education teachers indicated that the instructional procedures were effective, efficient, and were compatible with the activities and routines of the general education settings.

Jimenez, B. A, Browder, D. M., Spooner, F., & Dibiase, W. (2012). Inclusive inquiry science using peer-mediated embedded instruction for students with moderate intellectual disability. *Exceptional Children, 78,* 301–317. doi:10.1177/001440291207800303

> Researchers examined the effects of peer-mediated time-delay instruction to teach inquiry science and use of a knowledge chart to students with moderate intellectual disability in an inclusive setting. Six general education peers implemented an embedded constant time-delay procedure during three science units with 5 students with moderate intellectual disability. All 5 students increased the number of correct science responses across all science units. In addition, all peers were able to implement EI with high fidelity, while maintaining science grades at pre-intervention levels. High levels of social validity were reported by peers and teachers.

Bowman, J., McDonnell, J., Ryan, J., Coleman, O., Conradi, L., & Eichelberger, C. (in press). The effects of embedded instruction in teaching students with moderate and severe disabilities to solve word problems. *Focus on Autism and Other Developmental Disabilities*.

> Researchers utilized a multiple probe across participant design to evaluate the effects of a GE teacher-delivered multi-component EI mathematics intervention package on two main variables: (1) students' ability to solve simple word problems (2) generalization across people and materials and to untaught word problems. The data indicate that the embedded mathematics instructional package was effective in teaching students to (1) solve addition word problems with sums less than five and (2) to generalize to untaught word problems and across people and materials.

Ryan, J., Jameson, J.M., Coleman, O., Eichelberger, C., Bowman, J., Conradi, L., & Johnston, S. (In press). Inclusive social studies content instruction for students with significant intellectual disability using structured inquiry-based instruction. *Education and Training in Autism and Developmental Disabilities*.

> Researchers used a multiple probe across participants single case design was used to determine the effectiveness of paraprofessional-implemented inquiry-based social studies instruction, presented within an EI distribution schedule in general education classrooms. Study results suggest that this method of instruction had a positive effect on recall of information presented during history lessons for three junior high school students with intellectual disability. Initial explorations indicate that EI may provide an procedural framework for inclusive instruction using complex instructional interventions.

Appendix C: Peer Tutoring Training Script

I want to teach you how to embed instruction into the ongoing activities and routines of your general education class using a constant time-delay procedure. Before we get started, let's look at two of the terms used here and talk about them for a second.

Embed. To *embed instruction* simply means that we will teach, through one-to-one teaching, ceramics terms to Ella in her Arts and Crafts class. In order to do this, we want to be sure that we don't interrupt the usual activities in the class to complete Ella's teaching. The way we will avoid this is by embedding the teaching into times when both you and Ella do not have any demands from the teacher. For example, if the teacher is calling roll or taking time to hand back assignments that were graded, that might be a good time to do a couple of teaching trials. It would not be appropriate for you to teach Ella while the teacher was giving a lecture or demonstrating something to the class! Let's take some time to identify some good times for instruction:

Yes	No	Transitions (moving from one activity to another)
Yes	No	Parallel instruction
Yes	No	Teacher lecture time
Yes	No	Testing/assessment time
Yes	No	Free time
Yes	No	Independent activity

Other?_____

It will be up to you to decide when you will provide instruction during the class. It is very important, however, that in each class when you are teaching, you provide at least three trials for each of the items that Ella will be learning.

Constant time delay (CTD). Constant time delay is an instructional procedure that is both natural and intuitive. You used some of the steps already when you taught Ella before this training! It is easy to use and it is designed to ensure that students with disabilities get immediate feedback on the skills they are learning in a systematic and controlled way. It also ensures that they make very few errors while they are learning the material. The basic process is:

1. Select on opportunity to teach (remember ... three times per item in each class).
2. Get the student's attention.
3. Present the item to be learned (flash card).
4. Give teaching request.
5. Provide time for a response.

6. Provide feedback (zero-delay only).
7. Provide praise or correction.
8. Record data.

There are two types of delay: the zero-second time delay and the 3-second time delay. Let's look at both.

Zero-second time delay	
1. Select on opportunity to teach *Remember: At least three times per item in each class; choose times that do not cause disruption or distraction.*	
2. Get the student's attention.	"Ella, look at the card."
3. Present the item to be learned (flash card).	Show Ella the flash card.
4. Give teaching request.	"Ella, _____ means _____?"
5. Provide time for a response. *With zero-second delay, we don't provide any time. Provide the answer immediately. This makes sure that Ella does not make any errors yet.*	
6. Provide feedback.	Ella, _____ means _____." Example: "Ella, *wedging* means to mix clay." Tell her the correct answer and have her repeat it back to you exactly.
7. Provide praise or correction.	If Ella repeats the answer correctly, say, "Good job, Ella. That is right." If Ella does not repeat what you said, say, "No. Ella, _____ means _____."
8. Record the data.	Mark on the data collection sheet if her first response was correct (+) or not (-).
3-second time delay	
1. Select on opportunity to teach *Remember: At least three times per item in each class; choose times that do not cause disruption or distraction.*	
2. Get the student's attention.	"Ella, look at the card."
3. Present the item to be learned (flash card).	Show Ella the flash card.
4. Give teaching request.	"Ella, _____ means _____?"
5. Provide time for a response. *In this case you wait 3 seconds. This gives Ella time to respond.*	
6. Provide feedback.	"Ella, _____ means _____." Example: "Ella, *wedging* means to mix clay." Tell her the correct answer and have her repeat it back to you exactly.
7. Provide praise or correction.	If Ella repeats the answer correctly, say, "Good job, Ella. That is right." If Ella does not repeat what you said, say, "No. Ella, _____ means _____."
8. Record the data.	Mark on the data collection sheet if her first response was correct (+) or not (-).

Let's practice a few times. I will play Ella and you provide me with instruction.